To Dan,

A fine business associate,
sportsman, and friend —
Merry Christmas, 1978.

Duff

Waterfowling

HARPER & ROW, PUBLISHERS

New York, Hagerstown, San Francisco, London

Waterfowling

MONTE BURCH

FIRST EDITION

Designed by Lydia Link

Library of Congress Cataloging in Publication Data

Burch, Monte.
  Waterfowling.
  Includes index.
  1. Waterfowl shooting. I. Title.
SK331.B87 1977   799.2′44   74–1795
ISBN 0–06–010572–0

---

78 79 80 81 82 10 9 8 7 6 5 4 3 2 1

Contents

Acknowledgments

I wish to thank all the good people who have been kind enough to supply me with information and photos. And many thanks to all the waterfowlers I have had the privilege of hunting with and who have willingly shared their secrets. A special thanks to Bill Harper for his invaluable assistance, and to my wife Joan, for aiding me in putting together this labor of love.

Introduction

Waterfowling is an exhilarating experience that can be appreciated only by one who has spent a day in a marsh teeming with wildlife or has watched the sun rise above a rosy horizon to be lost in the vastness of open water and sky.

Waterfowling has been a great love of mine since I was a farm boy growing up in Missouri. With all the concentration and fervor of a twelve-year-old, I would stalk ducks that frequented the ponds and small twisting creeks near our farm. As I grew older, the magic of the marshes and river bottoms took on even more meaning, and I began to learn and understand more about life itself through my waterfowling adventures.

Today, all kinds of hunting are being threatened by well-meaning people who have completely lost touch with the natural world. These people live in a technological world where their very food—their sustenance—is so remote to them that eating a piece of beef or pork is merely an act of purchasing and preparing an impersonal, neatly cut and packaged product. And these are the same people who despise individuals who take their sustenance in a more natural way by hunting. But man *is* a predator. Our very existence depends on killing and eating other animals and plants. Hunting wild game is a natural extension of our inherited foraging instincts, and the hunter need make apologies to no one for the way he gets his food. The hunter is the most natural consumer.

Although many waterfowlers still hunt for the sake of putting food in their larder, many more go afield to escape the complicated world and to go back to the natural outdoors. Over 90 percent of man's time on this earth has been devoted to hunting and gathering food, and days spent in a pursuit like waterfowling give a man balance and a feeling of his true role and worth. The real hunter is a sensitive person, who becomes so involved with his quarry that he knows it almost as well as he does himself.

Yes, the waterfowler hunts for many reasons, but the most important is to become involved in the marshes and wetlands that ducks and geese call home. These areas are virtually teeming with wildlife. Very few moments are dull in a duck marsh, and the waterfowler learns to cherish each experience, from the breathtaking cold of icy water coming in over his boot-tops to the awe-inspiring scene of mallards or canvasbacks suddenly bursting through mist and fog on a gray day.

I have been lucky enough to experience the world of waterfowling with many fine men and women, and I hope I can pass along some of the excitement, fun, and fulfillment that I have gained from these adventures.

1

Duck Hunting

Duck hunting is a rich and a rewarding sport. It is very demanding, but gives much in return. Imagine yourself hunkered down in a reed-covered wooden blind on a cold November morning. The old plank seat is covered with a thick layer of frost, but you're snug and warm in your heavy clothes and waders, and you don't notice the cold except for your uncovered hands. In the first light of dawn the decoys are beginning to show, and you see distant groups of ducks wheeling and moving against the slowly brightening sky. You hear the rustling of wings somewhere as a flight passes behind you. One of your two companions checks his watch and whispers, "Shooting time in about four minutes." The three of you begin to watch the distant ducks more closely. In a few moments you spot a flight angling away from you but maybe just a little closer than most of the others. You raise the worn wooden call to your lips and blow a loud, confident, welcoming call to the fast-moving ducks. Do they hear you? Yes, they're banking into a turn in your direction. The ducks are moving so fast they're almost on you; they make a wide turn and pass around to your left and behind the blind. As they make their turn, you chuckle a feeding call. They come into sight, passing around the right side of the blind, necks craning and heads weaving back and forth as they cautiously examine the scene below them. They pass just out of range over the decoys and start to make another circle around the blind. You can see them clearly now—five drakes and seven hen mallards. The cream-colored bellies of the drakes are tinted a brilliant orange by the reflected sunrise as they wheel around the blind. They're lower this time, and you know they're going to come in, so you give one final feeding chuckle and stop. No one in the blind stirs now; everyone clutches his gun, eyes strained far to the right for the first look at the landing ducks. There they are—big red feet stuck wide out in front, powerful wings beating strongly to slow down for the descent into the opening that you've made in the decoys.

"Now!" you shout, and everyone raises and fires. You drop a startled drake with your first barrel but miss a second climbing fast to your left. Out of the corner of your eye you notice three others have dropped and are floating in the water. All green-head drakes—this is a moment to be proud of. Everything came together perfectly. The blind was situated and constructed properly, the decoys were set out right, you called as you

Duck hunting is one of the most rewarding outdoor sports. A day spent in a duck marsh or on the open sea gunning sea divers can provide drama and excitement but, most of all, a great appreciation and understanding of the natural world.

A caller brings a flight of mallards into a small pothole.

And a pair of drakes are dropped.

should, and even though you missed the second bird, the first was a one-shot kill. The quivering black Lab on the dog platform has already left the blind with his front feet, and you quickly give him his command. You'll forgive him his headstart this time; it's the first retrieve of the day, and you are as excited as he is. You smile as you catch your breath, realizing you have the entire day ahead to enjoy.

North American ducks nest and raise their young in the north, then fly south each year to winter. The successful waterfowler learns what kinds of ducks migrate through his area and what their major migration routes are. Ducks usually use the rivers as highways because of the abundance of lakes, sloughs, and waterways surrounding them. They will flock into almost any water area if there is sufficient food and it is in their migration path. The successful hunter gets out early, before the season begins, and reconnoiters the area with a good pair of binoculars. He looks primarily for places with lots of water, then food, and finally resting spots. Knowing the habits of the ducks he is hunting is very important for the waterfowler.

Ducks, like most birds and animals, follow a predictable course of feeding and resting. If a hunter knows what kinds of food a given duck is likely to eat and what sort of spot it is likely to rest in, he'll be prepared for some highly successful and exciting hunting.

SOME PREFERRED DUCK FOODS

Knowing the habits and food preferences of the ducks in your area can mean more successful hunting. These are some of the favorite foods of puddle ducks.

Acorns   Excellent; preferred by mallards, black ducks, and wood ducks.
Aneilema   Good for black ducks, pintails, and mallards.
Barnyard Grass   Good feed, well adapted to wet soils.
Buckwheat   A preferred food of puddle ducks; it is generally cultivated.
Bulrush   Very important food in the Gulf states.
Chufa   Excellent food for pintails and mallards.
Cockspur   Good; can grow in medium salinity.
Corn   Managed grain crop; a favorite with all puddle ducks.
Delta Arrowhead   Liked by canvasbacks, ring-necked ducks, mallards, and pintails; normally found only in lower Mississippi Gulf coast area.
Eelgrass   Favorite with divers; requires a current.
Flatsedge   Excellent duck food of the Gulf states.

Millet   Browntop, Japanese, German, wild, and Foxtail; all excellent
foods for mallards, pintails, and other puddle ducks.

Sawgrass   Seeds primarily eaten as grit.

Smartweeds   Excellent duck food; favorite of mallards.

Widgeongrass   Good duck food; requires brackish water.

Wild Rice   Excellent duck food of the South.

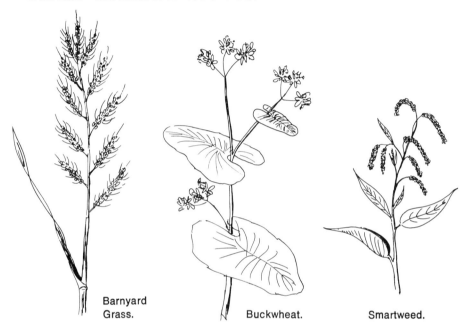

Barnyard
Grass.   Buckwheat.   Smartweed.

TYPES OF HUNTING

There are many kinds of duck hunting, and each requires a knowledge of special techniques. Ducks may be hunted over decoys in potholes, large open lakes and other waters, large river sandbars, and
flooded timber slashes. They may also be shot over decoys in dry or
flooded grain fields. Ducks are stalked for jump shooting, or by floating a
small river.

Pothole Shooting

The most popular type of puddle duck hunting is from potholes and
small sloughs. Shooting over decoys is the traditional and most common
method of duck hunting in the United States. Much of it is done on

These hunters are gunning from a grassed blind deep in a marsh-hay slough, a natural loafing spot for puddle ducks.

private lands and in shooting clubs, but with a little research, it's possible to discover some potholes and sloughs for yourself. The best shooting on these small waters will be near rivers, so one good way of locating them is to walk the riverbanks and watch for outflowing sloughs or places where the river might have rechanneled and left an oxbow lake.

The flats around the larger lakes are also good spots to look for sloughs and potholes. When these lakes flood, they cover the smaller surrounding potholes and marshes; as the flooding recedes, the smaller lakes are left with water that can provide some really great shooting. Examining a topographical map is useful, too, but remember—most pothole areas are on private property, so ask permission before trespassing.

Pothole, slough, and small pond shooting is most often done as the ducks pass from their river or marsh resting spots to feeding grounds early in the morning and late in the day. Potholes can easily be over-shot, and it's a good idea to shoot them only during the mornings, allowing the ducks to come back and use them for resting in the afternoons.

Potholes can yield extremely fine hunting if located near dry grain fields. The first thing an old mallard or pintail does after stuffing his crop with corn or grain is to look for a drink, and he will bail right on into a small pothole with a couple dozen decoys. I have often shot mallards so full of corn that the grain was falling right out of their mouths and it seemed incredible that they could even manage to fly.

Field Shooting

Naturally, field shooting is practiced most in the grainbelt areas, either in flooded or dry fields. With today's mechanical pickers a tremendous amount of grain is left scattered on the ground, and an old mallard will zoom in on it like a magnet. A mallard can eat up to 2 pounds of grain a day, and there's nothing they like better than fresh corn. With this knowledge a hunter who likes to spend a little time scouting the country can come up with some very exciting shooting. The trick is to look for grain fields near rivers, large lakes, or waterfowl refuges, then ask the owners for permission to hunt. Because of the popularity of this type of hunting there are many day-shooting blinds constructed for rental in these areas, particularly those near refuges or large lakes, so you may have to pay a fee. Even so, field shooting can be mighty economical if you find the right spot and get permission. All you need is about a dozen decoys, a camouflage net to hide under, plenty of shells, and a pair of hip waders or rubber boots.

Timber Shooting

Shooting mallards or pintails out of flooded timber is an experience that every waterfowler should have at least once. Puddle ducks love acorns, and they grow sleek and fat on them. Ducks seem to lose their inhibitions when they come into flooded timber and they'll dive straight into a handful of decoys even if the hunter is right there, leaning against a gnarled old oak or cypress tree.

In fact, a good method of attracting ducks in flooded timber is to kick the water with your boot, all the while blowing feeding chatter on your call. The sound simulates a flock of mallards noisily feeding on acorns and will bring in ducks you don't even see.

Half a dozen decoys are plenty for this type of shooting. Once the first mallard sees your decoys and starts dropping down through the trees, the rest of the flock will play follow-the-leader until the entire flight is funneling down into the tiny pothole. Judge Kelso of southwestern

DUCK HUNTING IN A FLOODED FIELD

With nothing more than an old sack for a blind, a lone hunter waits for mallards to come into the center of a cornfield.

High overhead, flight after flight of mallards circles the field of corn.

Finally they set their wings and come in.

Four drake mallards—and the end of a happy day of hunting a flooded grain field.

Some of the most fantastic duck hunting is in flooded timber, where mallards and pintails feed on acorns, one of their favorite foods.

Missouri and I once had over 1,000 mallards funnel in within 25 yards of us, and it was an experience neither of us will ever forget.

If you know the area pretty well, you can get by with wading; but if you're unfamiliar with it, it's best to move by boat rather than take the chance of hitting a deep hole and stepping in over your head.

Floating Rivers

Early in the season one of the best methods for taking ducks is to float down a small river. The ideal rivers for this purpose are tiny brush-tangled ones that snake through farming or grain country. Most puddle ducks feed early in the morning and late in the afternoon, and rest on rivers or large marshes the remainder of the day. Thus, floating down a river can be a great way of picking up some action during the middle of the day when the ducks aren't moving. Rivers are especially favorite resting spots for black ducks and mallards, and either one of these choice ducks can provide some mighty fast shooting as you surprise them on a river.

River drifting is best done from a camouflaged canoe or a small, lightweight johnboat. The best rivers have lots of log jams; since you'll have to pick up and portage over or around them, you should use as small a boat as you can get by with.

You can drift rivers by yourself or with a companion, but if two men are drifting, only the front man should be shooting. The stern man does all the paddling, allowing the bowman to sit still, watch for ducks, then take the shots. After each shot the paddlers change positions.

The idea is to drift with the current, making as little noise as possible and hoping to float up on resting or feeding ducks. Most ducks will be on the insides of bends, where there is quiet eddy water. The best method of surprising ducks is to drift up close to the inside of the bend, then come around quickly. Your shots will usually be at extremely close range but quite challenging because of the movement of the boat and the startling, noisy takeoff of the ducks. Even if you are prepared to see ducks around the bend, it's always a little unnerving when they do take off. It takes a good waterfowler to identify ducks in this situation and a good wing shot to bring them down. When ducks are flushed in this manner they usually

River hunting from a camouflaged canoe is particularly suitable early and late in the season when most of the smaller open waters have iced over.

head downstream a couple of hundred yards—so if you're careful you may get another chance at them. But they're much more wary by then, and it takes even more finesse to connect.

Shooting rivers can also be exciting when the season is just about at its end and most other waters have frozen over. You will usually have to walk the banks and find a good open spot near slow water. Place a half dozen decoys in this spot and you'll have some mighty great shooting.

A lot of hunters like to combine river drifting with shooting over decoys, and will drift until they find a good wide shoal or gravel bar near slow water, and then set up a small decoy spread. They shoot this for a while, then drift to another gravel bar, hunting as they go.

When putting out decoys in rivers, place them in slow backwater rather than in the current. Backwaters are logical places for ducks to land, and your decoys won't be carried away by the current.

Only fairly good rivermen should use either of these methods. An amateur may get a bad dunking, which in extremely cold weather could even be tragic.

If the river float is of any length, you should have a put-in point and a take-out point with a car at each end. Then you can spend the entire time floating new water, getting out when you reach your destination, rather than paddling back upstream to your car.

Shooting Over Open Water and Large Lakes

Gunning open water for divers and sometimes puddle ducks separates the waterfowling men from the boys and is one of the most challenging types of waterfowling. It requires the best in gear, expert boatmanship, a well-developed knowledge of duck habits, and good marksmanship. Open water shooting also requires large numbers of decoys—the more successful sets use several hundred.

This type of shooting is traditionally done in heavy seas, where the weather is naturally rough, along coastal bays and flats, or on large freshwater lakes. The game is primarily diving ducks, although some puddle ducks may also be attracted. Diving ducks will often feed all day, rafting up in good feeding areas and alternately feeding and resting. They prefer aquatic plants and will dive to great depths for them.

Surprisingly, some of our most populated inland lakes are feeding grounds for divers. Certain diving ducks ignore the human population around the lake if there's enough food and open water to stay clear of boaters. Many inland hunters don't realize there are such concentrations of ducks on nearby lakes. As a result, several state fish and game commissions allow extra seasons on these ducks, making some of them (such as

In the early morning light a lone hunter makes a deep water set, hoping for "Cans," bluebills, and maybe some blacks.

Hunters rise from a low-floating layout boat for a passing canvasback, the king of diver ducks.

scaup) bonus ducks, so you can take them in addition to the regular limit of puddle ducks.

Good lakes for gunning divers should have plenty of islands or rocky points to shoot from and plenty of deep flats with lots of food.

Jump Shooting

Jump shooting—sneaking up on resting or feeding ducks, then jumping up to scare them into the air for shots—is the way many Midwestern farm kids learn their duck hunting. Though it is extremely effective, it can be unsporting unless the shooter chooses his shots.

Jump shooting is a good method during the heat of the day when most waterfowl are resting. Then the hunter can stalk the small ponds, sloughs, old quarries, coal strip pits, or even small streams, walking the banks with a good retriever to flush ducks that may be sitting in close to the overhanging river cover.

Unfortunately, too many hunters jump shoot in quite another way. They drive around the countryside in an automobile until they spot ducks on a pond; then without asking permission they crawl over a fence, sneak up on the ducks, and blast them while they sit on the water. This is what makes jump shooting unsportsmanlike. As both a sportsman and landowner I have seen this type of "hunt" happen too often.

One great way to duck hunt in the middle of the day when the action slows down is to sneak hunt the potholes, farm ponds, river sloughs, and strip pits.

Pass Shooting

Pass shooting is a method of shooting birds as they pass over high spots or regularly used trading areas between feeding and resting grounds. It can demand good marksmanship but also tends to promote "sky-busting" and is in my opinion the least desirable method of hunting waterfowl. To be sure, on some days it may be the only way of bringing in game; but the chances of leaving cripples are just too great.

Each type of hunting is more effective at certain times and in certain situations. A good waterfowler knows when to use each. Regardless of method, the name of the game is to get out in the marshes or water and shoot ducks. In the next few chapters we will go into further detail on boats, guns, decoys, and specific blinds for different shooting situations.

Duck and goose hunting can amount to a lot more than just shooting ducks and geese. It can be a birdwatcher's dream. Concealed in the blind, you may see anything from a great blue heron to a big buck deer to a bald eagle picking up a crippled duck. One blustery cold day a couple of years ago three of us were hunkered deep in a concrete water blind in a flooded timber slash. We had collected one mallard each and were softly talking, watching the sky and waiting for another flight, when a tiny Carolina wren perched on one of the branches covering the front opening of the blind. The little wren wasn't 2 feet from anyone in the blind, and she confidently started to pick the branch free of grubs. Her perky little tail and quick nervous movements brought smiles to all our faces, and no one moved when a group of blue-winged teal buzzed the blind several times, then alighted in the decoys.

2

Goose Hunting

There is something exciting and primitive about the distant honking of geese, passing high overhead in the gray clouds of an autumn sky. It reminds us of far-off places and suggests the coming beauty of autumn and the inevitable solitude of winter. When I was growing up in Missouri, the cries of geese always announced an exciting change of pace. Our entire family would rush out and watch the flights as they winged their way south, knowing it was time to start putting up food in earnest for the cold winter months ahead.

To the waterfowler the cries of these majestic birds bring thoughts of cold dark mornings when he eagerly awaits the dawn, and of huge flights of geese rising from their night-time resting water with a roar of wings and a confused gabble that can be heard for miles.

Hunting the big Canadas, snows, and blues is the ultimate experience for many waterfowlers. These birds are considered the finest game and are the most popular species hunted in North America. The Canada goose in flight, the symbol of all U.S. national wildlife refuges, represents the beauty, excitement, and skill of the true waterfowling sport.

One of the most challenging aspects of hunting geese is that it usu-

To many waterfowlers the Canada goose is the king of birds. Hunting this majestic and intelligent creature can provide some of life's most exciting moments.

ally requires a tremendous amount of effort to hunt them successfully, unless you rent a private blind near a public hunting refuge or can secure a blind for a day on a public hunting refuge.

Probably the most popular method of goose hunting is shooting from blinds over decoys, either in grain fields or over open water, large river sandbars, or large sloughs and marshes.

Sneak hunting and pass shooting are less popular methods. Both can be extremely effective, but unfortunately they are too often practiced in an unsportsmanlike manner that is contemptible to the true waterfowler.

REFUGE HUNTING

Most goose hunting today is done on public hunting lands in refuges managed primarily for waterfowl. Each year these giant refuges attract hundreds of thousands of waterfowl and thousands of gunners.

At the beginning of the season, gunning geese on these huge refuges is all too easy. The migrating flocks are attracted to the area by the tremendous amount of grain planted to feed them, and they are quite reluctant to leave, regardless of the shooting pressure. Consequently, on the larger, more populated refuges there is a quota of geese that can be shot each year; when it is reached, all goose shooting must stop in the immediate area of the refuge and surrounding private lands.

But as the season progresses, the birds grow much more wary and shooting can become extremely frustrating as thousands of geese mill and swarm just out of gun range. This results in many unsportsmanlike shooting practices, particularly sky-busting—or shooting at geese that are out of gun range. Shooting at geese that are barely in range is even worse,

HUNTERS' FAVORITE GEESE

The snow and its cousin the blue goose are favorite targets for goose hunters.

Canada geese are another hunters' favorite. Here, taking off, Giant Canadas show the distinguishing white crescent mark on the backs of their tails.

A hunter scans the horizon for signs of geese leaving a refuge area and heading out to feed late in the afternoon.

being more likely to cripple than kill cleanly. It takes a lot of shot to bring down a big old goose. The number one rule of a compassionate and sportsmanlike hunter is to shoot only at geese within range.

Unfortunately, it's pretty hard for anyone, whether beginner or skilled old-timer, to tell exactly when geese are within clean killing range. One method used by sharp-eyed hunters is to hold their fire until they can clearly see the goose's eye. The best answer is to set your decoys at a close range, around 35 yards, and only fire when the geese are slowly settling down into them. You have fewer cripples with this method because you're shooting at the softer feathers on the underside, rather than the back and wing feathers, which can deflect a lot of shot.

Of course when you're pass shooting, only experience can determine the proper shooting distance, and that can vary from person to person, depending on the size of shot, bore of gun, etc.

Because of the tremendous numbers of waterfowl and hunters, the public hunting areas on the refuges are strictly managed, and hunters should be sure to familiarize themselves with local rules and regulations, copies of which are generally available on request.

The private lands close to wildlife refuges are usually completely covered with blinds that can be rented, often at exorbitant costs, by the day, week, or season. They are generally filled each day until the season

A flight of passing geese about 40 yards away displays the usual V-formation, shifting and reshifting to allow each goose a chance to rest.

quotas are reached. These blinds provide "pass shooting," as geese by the thousands leave the refuges to feed in the early morning and late afternoon.

Hunting unmanaged private and public lands is very different from hunting the highly mechanized shooting galleries called wildlife refuges. Setting up your own hunting requires a tremendous amount of work, equipment, and time, a real knowledge of goose habits, and not a little money. The results more than make up for the effort, however, when you meet the wary and intelligent goose on a more equal footing.

It's one thing to walk into a goose blind already set with several hundred decoys and located in a good goose hunting area. It's quite another when you've got to hunt up and scout out an area yourself, get permission to hunt, then carry several hundred goose decoys for a mile or two through gumbo mud, dig in a blind, and arrange your decoys—all before the break of dawn on a day that's usually cold, wet, and icy. With all your work done you watch the coming dawn with intense anticipation, straining for the sound of geese in the distance.

Geese are the "big game" of waterfowl, so hunting them is highly regulated—often restricting the hunter to one hunt a year. Hunters here are bringing geese into a check station. Biologists will determine age, sex, and weight—all important factors in goose management.

FIELD HUNTING

Field shooting geese over decoys is probably the most popular form of goose shooting, and it is the one most often practiced by the true sportsman-waterfowler. There are several ways of going about this.

Somewhat like homing pigeons, geese return to the same places each year, using practically the exact migration pattern. If you're lucky enough to own or lease land near these migration routes, some of the world's finest shooting can be yours. If you don't happen to live near a migration route where the best hunting spots are pretty well known, you'll have to get out and scout around to locate good goose hunting areas, which can be harder to find than good duck hunting areas. Ducks tend to stay in one place for a fairly long period, and their migration pattern is usually protracted, with small groups continually coming and going. Goose migrations, however, are very concentrated, and geese can arrive at and then leave an area within a very short time, particularly if the flock is large and the food scarce. Thus, locating prime goose hunting areas is very tricky. Many places that look like truly fine goose hunting grounds may never be visited by geese because of their strict adherence to traditional migration routes. Also, pre-season scouting by watching local geese will in no way help you to determine the flight route of migrants.

The most accepted practice in field shooting, unless you own or lease a blind in a well-traveled migration route, is to scout the reserves, refuges, or large bodies of open water such as inland lakes or bays for nesting geese. Early in the morning, watch for the huge flights of geese leaving the water. They may fly 15 or 20 miles to feed. Follow them in a car until you spot their feeding areas. Watch as the geese feed, and then ask permission from the farmer or landowner to hunt the field that afternoon or the next day. Hunting as soon as possible after determining the feeding area is extremely important. Many landowners will gladly grant permission because huge flocks of grazing geese can literally destroy entire crops in a short time if the grain hasn't been harvested.

Mechanical grainpickers, which drop large amounts of grain, are a major factor in today's increasing number of geese. Geese dearly love grain, especially the early sprouts of winter wheat, barley, and rye. They also like the grain that has been dropped in freshly picked fields of corn, soybeans, wheat, and barley.

Geese are extremely wary and will often circle for several minutes, carefully examining every particle of the field below them before finally settling down in the center to eat. Then they will leave a sentry or two on

Bill Harper puts out a set of profile goose decoys in a flooded soybean field.

high ground constantly watching. If there is any sign of danger the sentry will immediately give the alarm, the entire flock will become dead silent, stick their necks straight up, and wait for further signs. If they spot you, the entire flock will bunch up and take off with a great cackling and rustling of wings.

Once a feeding field has been located and permission to hunt granted, the real work begins. Geese will not come near any type of obstacle or unusual landmark in an otherwise flat grain field, and they usually stay so close to the center of large fields that shooting from the surrounding fence lines or brush is impossible.

There are several methods of hunting these fields. If it is early in the season and the birds haven't become too gun-shy, you can lie on the ground and cover yourself with a dead-grass camouflage net or stalks of the freshly picked grain. If there are patches of snow on the ground, you can cover yourself with an old sheet, leaving eyeholes to watch for birds coming into your decoys. It takes a really dedicated goose hunter to withstand the rigors of this type of hunting, because the cold wet ground can quickly chill you, and you may have a long wait before you get a chance to shoot. In the latter part of the season, however, even this ruse will not work on the cautious birds.

In this case you will have to dig a pit to shoot from. This too involves a great deal of work, and you should always inform the landowner of your intentions and refill the pit after you use it. All dirt from the pit should be mounded up around it and covered with stalks, or, even better, moved to the sides of the field. If the fresh dirt is merely spread out around the pit, it will make a large circular pattern that is easily recognized from the air. Cover the top with a screen camouflaged with grain stalks. These pits require a lot of work, but if they are built in the morning they may be used for the afternoon shoot. If the pit is in an extremely promising area and you can obtain a lease, you may wish to install the blind permanently. (Plans and instructions for these permanent pit blinds are given in Chapter 6.)

Geese normally use the larger river systems as primary migration routes, so the large marshes, deltas, and flood plains of rivers like the Missouri, Mississippi, and Platt are good places for goose hunting. Extensive marshlands with large grain fields nearby, and large bodies of open water within easy flying distance, almost guarantee great goose shooting.

Since geese are so easily spooked, careful blind setting, good decoy spreads, the removal of any bright object from the blind area, and an immobile pose by everyone in the blind, will all be necessary in order to bring the geese within gun range.

FIELD HUNTING

Goose hunting can be very demanding, particularly in the fields.

A day in the fields means tolerating the cold, wet gumbo mud that sticks to everything and makes your feet weigh a ton.

One of the most challenging methods of hunting geese is to crawl on your belly, trying to sneak up on them as they feed in an open field.

A gunner in a field lines up on a flight of Canadas.

Success—a gunner has dropped a big old gander from a flock of decoying Canadas.

A hardworking black Lab brings back a goose that landed in flooded timber.

Sneak Shooting

Some hunters like to use the same scouting techniques mentioned above for locating fields of feeding geese and then stalk the birds. Geese traditionally pick fields for feeding that are as flat and open as possible, and they can see any movement for an incredible distance.

Successfully stalking a flock of geese on your hands and belly through muck and mud, then knocking down one of the fast-flying, startled birds, is a feat that requires the best in stalking skill and in patience. The keen eyesight and wary intelligence of these birds make this type of hunting extremely challenging and rewarding.

Try the method used by Indian hunters in stalking game. Carefully watch the sentinel geese. As soon as they look away from you, move a few feet closer, swimming in the mud and keeping as low to the ground as possible. If the sentinels or other geese in the flock quickly bunch up or stick their heads up high on straight necks, lie as still as possible until they resume their feeding. This truly takes patience, as you may have to play a waiting game for half an hour or more. To make such a stalk you should carefully plot out each move, using binoculars to study the terrain before you begin. It can be very frustrating to crawl 100 yards through icy mud, only to find that you can't crawl the remaining 50 to get within gun range. It is also a good idea to glass the area carefully for other hunters, because it is equally frustrating to make a long stalk only to have another hunter jump and start shooting just as you get halfway to the feeding flock.

You should watch for the general direction in which the flock is feeding. As a large flock of geese feed, they have a tendency to move in one direction. If possible you should try to make your stalk so that they will be feeding toward you.

One method of stalking geese is deplorable and deserves no discussion—using a four-wheel-drive automobile to chase them from field to field as they try to feed.

Pass Shooting

Pass shooting is normally done on the fringes of the big refuges in the areas geese use as traveling lanes between their feeding grounds and resting waters. Very few hunters can visualize the range of a high-flying goose. Consequently, pass shooting usually does nothing but encourage sky-busting.

On the other hand, it can provide some exciting gunning if the weather is very bad and the geese are staying in low to the ground. When the weather is stormy, geese will gain no more altitude than is absolutely necessary to clear the terrain. In this situation goose hunters can have some fabulous shooting, especially from the low saddles between ridges that geese must pass through on their travel lanes.

Shooting Over Water

Shooting geese over water is probably the most exacting form of goose hunting. It requires meticulous attention to every detail of blind site, decoy spread, and water condition.

Particularly if they're well camouflaged, most blinds set for ducks in large bodies of water will also work for geese. The trick is to place both goose and duck decoys. Snows and blues will not usually come into water sets as readily as Canadas.

Just as in shooting over fields, the main idea is not to put too much shooting pressure on the geese. Watch for the areas they're using; then when they leave early in the morning, set out your decoys and shoot the birds as they return from feeding.

Any extensive open water areas such as bays, sandbars on large rivers, and the shallows of large inland lakes (especially if there are grain fields nearby) are great places for water goose hunting.

One important note: decoys used in water sets must be kept in perfect condition and should float properly. Even one poorly placed or wobbly decoy can spook an entire flight of geese.

Brant Shooting

There are two distant species of the Brant family: the American Brant, found along the Atlantic coast, and the Black Brant, found along the Pacific. The Brant is a small dark goose similar to the Canadian except that it lacks the distinctive white cheek patch and has a dark, rather than light, chest. The Black Brant has a dark belly. A mature Brant also has a white neck ring that is not always easy to make out. Because of the Brant's very limited range, hunting for these geese is the choice of only a few dedicated shooters.

The Brant's flight is usually rapid, low over the water, and strung out, and they make a soft "kr---onk" sound. They eat aquatic plants, mostly eelgrass, which they get by "tipping up" or ducking under the water for. At one time these birds were almost extinct because of the loss of eelgrass and the destruction of their habitat, but they are gradually making a comeback, and Brant shooting is now allowed on a closely managed basis on both coasts.

Brant are birds of the saltwater bays and tidal flats. They spend most of their time offshore, coming in just to feed, which presents the only opportunity for gunning them.

Brant are usually gunned over decoys in much the same way as Canadian geese. It takes a good number of decoys to bring in a flight of Brant, and a couple hundred isn't too many. Blinds should be located near eelgrass feeding areas. For shooting Brant, it's best to use floating, stake, or boat blinds, located offshore between rafting Brant and their favorite feeding grounds.

Decoying geese over water is the most demanding method of bringing waterfowl into decoys.

♂

♀

3

Waterfowl Identification

Have you ever been with a guide or seasoned duck hunter who suddenly squints at the horizon and says softly, "Mallards just coming off the river"? Look as hard as you can, and you probably can't even spot a flight, let alone tell what kind of duck he's watching. Does he have some sort of built-in radar that lets him know where the ducks are and what kind? No, but he has developed a "duck knowledge" from many days of keen watching and studying. He's also probably the one shooter in your blind who consistently collects drakes only.

You too can learn to identify waterfowl, even at great distances. Certainly, no one would say that it's easy or that it doesn't take many hours of practice, but it is a lot of fun. This skill not only makes your day afield much more rewarding and interesting, but in today's regulated hunting it's almost a necessity. Selective shooting is the order of the day for the modern waterfowler, and it requires not only a good knowledge of the different species of ducks and geese, but the ability to recognize the differences between the sexes as well.

Reading a book won't make you an expert waterfowl identifier. To become truly expert, you've got to get out in the marsh and observe

Some species, such as these wood ducks, are rare in certain areas, and waterfowl identification is important to their preservation.

ducks and geese. Take a pair of binoculars and a good field guide with you, and really learn; it's well worth it.

One fun way of learning is to visit the waterfowl refuges in your area during the spring migrations. Check with your local fish and game departments to find out which areas are open to observation, then spend some time watching the different species. This is also a good time to listen to "marsh talk" and learn a little "duck language."

Many states use the point system to regulate the annual duck kill. This system, although somewhat more complicated than previous ones, allows the states to adapt their laws and regulations better to local bird populations.

By the point system you are limited to, say, 100 points a day. A hen mallard might count 90 points, a drake 25 or 20 points, a wood duck 100

With today's highly restricted point system of waterfowl management, identification becomes doubly important. Shooting one high-point duck such as this hen mallard could mean a limit.

points, and so forth. In some states you are allowed 100 points plus one duck, giving you a chance for a mistake if, for instance, you already have two drake mallards and accidentally kill a hen. In other states the scoring might be 90 points for a canvasback, a diminishing species, while blue-bills or scaup might rate 10 points.

A waterfowler has to be especially careful at the beginning of the fall, when early migrants such as teal are being hunted. At this time many waterfowl are in their "ellipse phase," meaning they are not fully feathered and are extremely hard to identify.

Whether or not your state has the point system, you'll come out ahead by knowing how to identify ducks and geese. First of all, many species are on the protected list and therefore must not be shot. Secondly, knowing your ducks can add an extra thrill to your day; you can collect "bonus" ducks or extra ducks that are overabundant in certain areas. Knowing your waterfowl pays off at the table too. Being able to tell a corn-fat mallard from a fish-eating merganser can mean the difference between a fine, satisfying meal and a dish so unpalatable that even your dog won't touch it.

There are seven basic identifying characteristics in waterfowl. Learn the characteristics of the waterfowl that normally inhabit your area, and you'll have a much more enjoyable and rewarding day afield.

Silhouette   Characteristic outline of the duck.
Flight Pattern   Fast or slow wingbeat; head up or down; etc.
Color Pattern   Distinctive pattern and/or colors that are easy to identify. (These may be hard to spot in poor weather conditions.)
Flock Action   Slow, direct, straight line; a weaving V; an erratic, twisting flight; etc.
Sound   Whistling wings; quacking; etc.
Landing and Taking Off   Fast, slow, springing up immediately, etc.
Habitat   Although it may vary different times of the year, most ducks stick pretty much to the particular habitat that suits their specific needs.

You may not be able to identify waterfowl positively by any one characteristic, but by noting several an easily recognizable pattern of the species can be determined.

IDENTIFYING DUCKS

There are two major classifications of ducks: puddle ducks and divers.

Puddle Ducks

Normally found in shallow freshwater marshes and small streams and lakes, puddle ducks are also called "dabblers" or surface-feeding ducks because they feed on water plants or waste corn or millet. These include mallards, pintails, gadwalls, and teal. Puddle ducks ride higher in the water than the bay and sea ducks, or divers; and when they take off from the water, they rise straight up with a fast leap and quick wing-beats. They have larger wings in relation to their body size than the divers. The speculum or secondary wing feathers of puddle ducks show an iridescent color in flight.

A good quick way to distinguish between dabblers and divers is by the shape of the foot. Puddle ducks have a small hind toe, and divers have a large, lobed hind toe. Although they are good divers, puddle ducks usually tip up or dabble rather than dive for their food.

When coming in to decoys, puddle ducks have a tendency to tease and torment. They may make up to a half dozen passes at your decoys before deciding to come on in, or they may turn on the tenth pass and head for safer country. It's generally helpful in recognizing ducks to learn how the different species approach your decoys. By the way, being a good caller helps bring a puddle duck in. You need to know when to call and when to keep still.

Since states are now using the point system, identifying birds in the blind after they have been shot is a necessity.

HUNTERS' GUIDE FOR DUCK IDENTIFICATION

Courtesy of Department of Interior, Fish and Wildlife Service

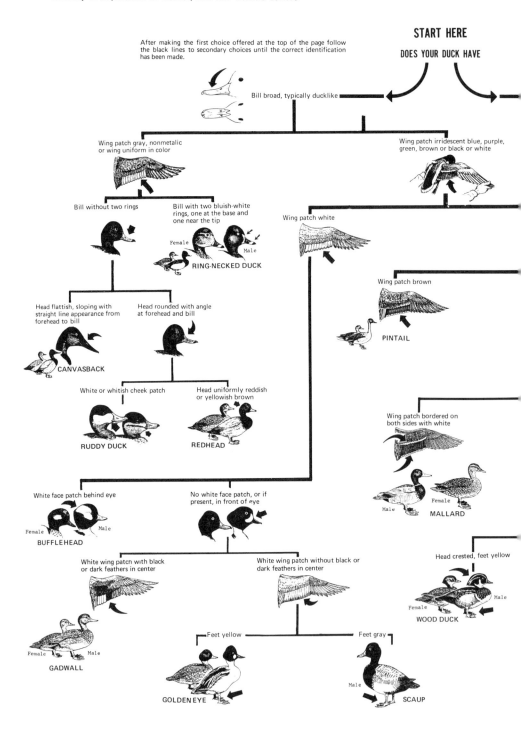

After making the first choice offered at the top of the page follow the black lines to secondary choices until the correct identification has been made.

START HERE

DOES YOUR DUCK HAVE

Bill broad, typically ducklike

Wing patch gray, nonmetalic or wing uniform in color

Wing patch irridescent blue, purple, green, brown or black or white

Bill without two rings

Bill with two bluish-white rings, one at the base and one near the tip

Wing patch white

Female   Male

RING-NECKED DUCK

Wing patch brown

PINTAIL

Head flattish, sloping with straight line appearance from forehead to bill

Head rounded with angle at forehead and bill

CANVASBACK

White or whitish cheek patch

Head uniformly reddish or yellowish brown

Wing patch bordered on both sides with white

RUDDY DUCK

REDHEAD

Male   Female

MALLARD

White face patch behind eye

No white face patch, or if present, in front of eye

Female   Male

BUFFLEHEAD

Head crested, feet yellow

Female   Male

WOOD DUCK

White wing patch with black or dark feathers in center

White wing patch without black or dark feathers in center

Female   Male

GADWALL

Feet yellow

Feet gray

GOLDENEYE

Male

SCAUP

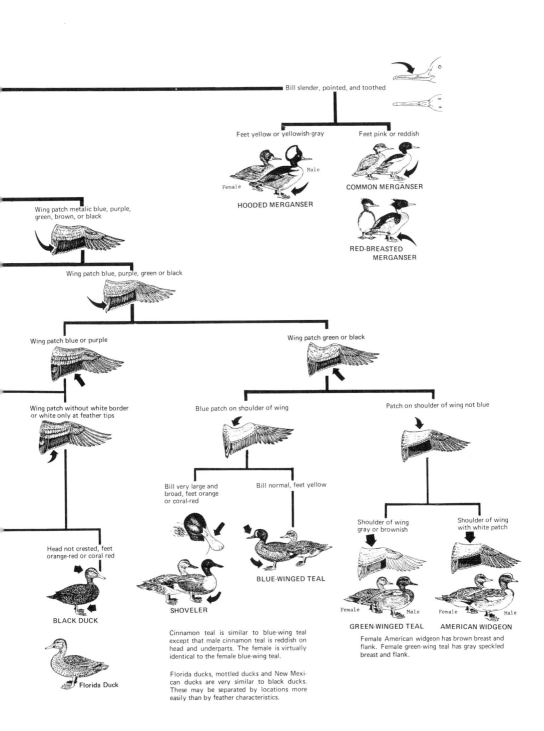

Bill slender, pointed, and toothed

Feet yellow or yellowish-gray

Feet pink or reddish

COMMON MERGANSER

HOODED MERGANSER

RED-BREASTED
MERGANSER

Wing patch metalic blue, purple,
green, brown, or black

Wing patch blue, purple, green or black

Wing patch blue or purple

Wing patch green or black

Wing patch without white border
or white only at feather tips

Blue patch on shoulder of wing

Patch on shoulder of wing not blue

Bill very large and
broad, feet orange
or coral-red

Bill normal, feet yellow

Shoulder of wing
gray or brownish

Shoulder of wing
with white patch

Head not crested, feet
orange-red or coral red

BLUE-WINGED TEAL

BLACK DUCK

SHOVELER

Florida Duck

Cinnamon teal is similar to blue-wing teal
except that male cinnamon teal is reddish on
head and underparts. The female is virtually
identical to the female blue-wing teal.

Florida ducks, mottled ducks and New Mexi-
can ducks are very similar to black ducks.
These may be separated by locations more
easily than by feather characteristics.

GREEN-WINGED TEAL   AMERICAN WIDGEON

Female American widgeon has brown breast and
flank. Female green-wing teal has gray speckled
breast and flank.

SEVEN IDENTIFYING CHARACTERISTICS OF WATERFOWL

Silhouette. The outline, or silhouette, of the duck is its most obvious and distinguishing characteristic. Here, a mallard drake is silhouetted.

Flight Pattern. The pattern of each species' flight is also important. Do they fly with fast or slow wingbeats? Do they hold their heads up or down? This pair of mallards, a drake (top) and a hen, illustrates their particular style of flight.

Color Pattern. Most waterfowl have an easily recognized area that is distinctly colored and identifies the species. For instance, the speculum or wing patch on most puddle ducks is brightly colored and iridescent. On bay or sea ducks the wing patch is usually duller, but it is still an important field mark for identification.

Flock Action. Some birds have a definite group action in flight that is easily recognized, like the follow-the-leader style of these mergansers.

Sound. Sound is another important identifying feature. Many ducks make specific noises while in flight. It may be the distinctive "kehonking" of Canadas, or the in-flight rustle of a whistling bluebill's wings.

Landing and Taking Off. The way a bird takes off from the water or lands is also an important identifying characteristic. Does it spring into the water, like a mallard, or patter along the surface gaining altitude slowly, like a canvasback?

Habitat. The type of habitat a duck uses can tell you as much as what the bird itself looks like.

THE NORTH AMERICAN FLYWAYS

There are four distinct flyways, each populated primarily by particular species of ducks, although there is, of course, some overlap.

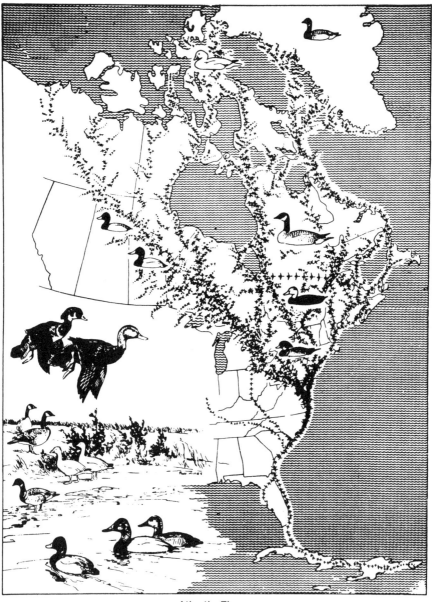

Atlantic Flyway

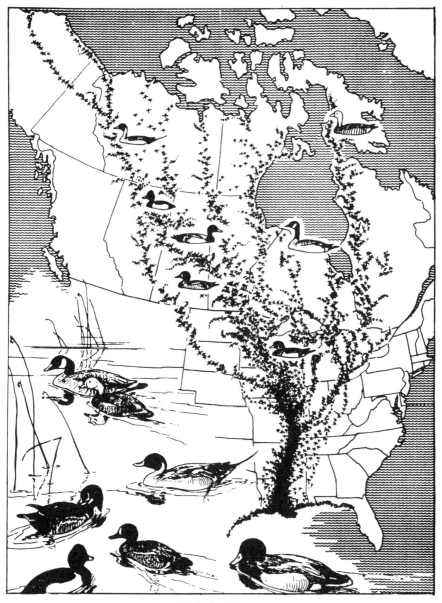

Mississippi Flyway

Central Flyway

Pacific Flyway

DISTINGUISHING PUDDLE DUCKS AND DIVERS

Puddle ducks, such as this pintail drake (left), ride relatively high in the water. Diver ducks, such as the scaup (right) sit low in the water and at a distance appear smaller than puddle ducks.

When puddle ducks take off (right), they jump out of the water with a mighty splash of wings and gain altitude rapidly. Divers (below) must run across the water for some distance before their smaller wings can give them the lift they need to gain altitude.

Puddle ducks (left) are also called dabblers, because their surface-feeding technique is to "dabble" and tip down to grasp seeds and other surface foods. Divers (below) plunge beneath the surface for food; many of them can dive to considerable depths for fish and other edibles.

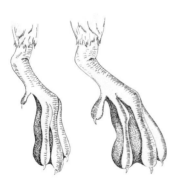

Puddle ducks (left) have small hind toes, while divers (right) have larger, lobed hind toes.

Puddle ducks (left) have relatively larger wings in relation to their bodies than divers (right), and they show bright color speculums on their wings.

Divers

There are two classes of diving ducks: bay ducks and sea ducks. Both types completely submerge when diving for food. The diving ducks inhabit coastal areas, bays, inlets, and larger rivers and deep lakes.

Dividing ducks have a more rapid wingbeat than puddle ducks because their wings are smaller in relation to their bodies. They also have shorter tails and duller speculums. Even in flight, they use their huge feet as rudders, so when you see a duck flying with large trailing feet, you've got yourself a good quick identification mark. The divers' method of launching into flight is also characteristic. Most of these ducks have to run along the surface of the water to gain enough speed for a takeoff.

Divers often plunge to great depths for food. Some have been known to go as deep as 200 feet, and they commonly try to escape danger by diving and swimming great distances underwater.

Because most of the divers feed on shellfish and mollusks, they are usually not quite as tasty as the puddle ducks. Canvasbacks and redheads, however, feed primarily on wild celery and eelgrass when they can get it and are excellent table birds.

When divers are coming in to decoys, they have a tendency to plunge right on in. But they closely scrutinize everything as they come and will sometimes pull out at the very last minute, making for some extremely exciting pass shooting.

IDENTIFYING GEESE

Distinguishing geese from ducks is not really difficult. When they're at a distance, though, and you're not sure whether to use a duck or goose call, it becomes extremely important to be able to identify them quickly.

As a rule, geese fly in some sort of formation, which may be a perfect V or a wavering line. Sometimes the birds may switch positions, making it hard to spot the formation, but usually there's a definite flight pattern.

Geese tend to fly higher than ducks, sometimes as high as 4,000 feet. The wingbeats of geese are much slower than those of ducks, although the birds are in fact moving quite fast. These deceptive wingbeats are often the undoing of the novice goose hunter. Watching the slow-moving, apparently heavy birds, the beginner underestimates their speed and shoots way behind them.

Silhouette is, of course, important. Geese have longer necks than ducks, and their wings tend to appear larger and more fan-shaped. Their

Distinguishing geese from ducks is not normally too much of a problem. The great size of geese and their vocal chatter, which can be seen and heard for miles, makes every waterfowler's heart beat just a little faster.

legs are placed closer to the center of their body front to back, making it easier for them to walk on land.

Like puddle ducks, geese spring into the air from the water and can leave it almost as fast as mallards. Because they are very talkative in flight, one quick way of identifying them is by the familiar honking made by members of the flight as they gabble their way toward you.

Geese make up their minds about landing from some distance. When they decide everything is Okay, they begin to set those wings and come in slowly but surely, giving everyone in the blind a bad case of the shakes.

DUCKS

WOOD DUCK

The drake wood duck is the most beautiful North American duck. Its head is black with iridescent greens, and it has a large black and white crest. The chest is burgundy flecked with white. Wood ducks are most often recognized in flight by the black back, white belly, and white chin patch extending up behind the eyes. They fly in a fast, direct manner,

Wood Duck.

♂

♀

often twisting their heads from side to side. The bill is usually pointed down. Flocks are small. Wood ducks are most often found along slow-moving creeks and streams, where they nest and winter. The species is becoming somewhat rare in many parts of the United States and should not be shot until their numbers increase. The population decline is due largely to loss of habitat as small streams have been gobbled up by numerous dams, and marshlands drained for cattle grazing and suburban real estate development. The drakes call "hoooooooooelt" in flight, and the hens make a soft, high quack.

MALLARD

The mallard, found in all flyways, is the most common duck in North America. It is a large and extremely hardy bird, often wintering as far north as it can find open water. If mallards have fed on corn, millet, or other cropland, they are one of the finest table birds. The drake's distinctive green head and rust chest, white neck ring, and white belly are easily

♂

♀

Mallard.

recognized. Mallards usually leave the rivers or lakes early in the morning and then again in late afternoon to feed in grain fields or flooded timberlands. They are one of the most vocal ducks. In flight the drake makes the familiar loud quacking sound; when feeding, it makes a low, gurgling chuckle. The hen often makes single soft quacks while on water. Giving these single, slow soft quacks on your duck call will often bring in a flight of wary late season mallards when nothing else will.

PINTAIL

Pintails are found in all flyways but are most prevalent in the West and some parts of the South. Extremely fast fliers, pintails are fond of swooping in from great heights to level off just short of landing. They have long necks, and the drake has a long black "pin" tail and a dark cinnamon brown head. The wing patch on both male and female is metallic green, with a buff strip at the top and a white strip below. The female does not have the long tail feathers. Both have gray bills and dark gray underwings. The breast is creamy white on the male, light buff on the female. Drake pintails utter a sharp low whistle; hens often make soft quacking sounds.

Pintail.

CINNAMON TEAL

The male is a dark red cinnamon, with light gray wing patches similar to those of the blue-winged teal. In flight the cinnamon teal is very similar to the blue-winged teal, and it is almost impossible to tell the females of the two species apart. Cinnamon teal, however, rarely fly in large groups

Cinnamon Teal.

as do blue-winged teal; they're normally seen only in pairs or singly. A very trusting bird, the cinnamon teal is extremely slow to alarm. Although a quiet species, the drakes sometimes make a low chatter and the hens a faint quack. Cinnamon teal are rare east of the Rocky Mountains.

GREEN-WINGED TEAL

A hardy bird, the green-winged teal sometimes stays as far north in winter as open water can be found. The male is a small dark brown duck, with a vertical white bar separating the spotted buff chest from the gray sides; the female is mottled brown and white. In spring a metallic green swatch extends from the eye to the nape of the neck in both sexes, giving the bird its name. Their flight is always swift and erratic, all members twisting and circling as a unit. They are sometimes found in large flocks. The green-winged teal nests as far north as Alaska and migrates south through all flyways. The drakes whistle and twitter; the hens have a slight quack.

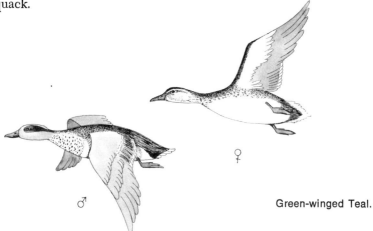

Green-winged Teal.

Blue-winged Teal.

BLUE-WINGED TEAL

This duck flies very, very fast in small, compact flocks. Because it's an early migrator, the blue-winged teal is sometimes seen still in the "ellipse" or molting phase before it has fully feathered, so that the drakes appear very similar to the hens The drake, however, has a dark belly whereas the hen has a light one. The easily seen blue patch on the forewing is often recognized in the field; the iridescent speculum wing patches are dark green. In flight the males appear to be mostly dark with a white crescent above the eye. Blue-winged teal fly in a twisting, dodging pattern through trees and brush. They make a soft whistling call while in flight. They are excellent small table birds.

SHOVELER

The most recognizable feature of this duck is its large spoon-shaped bill. Both sexes have a blue wing patch, and the drake has a dark green head, brown belly, and sides. The shoveler flies in erratic patterns in small flocks, and usually migrates early. The drake makes a "tucka-tucka-tucka"

Shoveler.

sound, the hen a soft quack. This duck is one of the least tasty because it is a bottom feeder, eating primarily crustaceans strained through the marsh mud by its enormous bill.

GADWALL

Both sexes of gadwall may be mistaken on the water for the female mallard. The speculum, however, is the gadwall's distinguishing mark; it is white with a dark streak through it, and a chestnut line on the top. The male is a dark gray bird with a brown head and black chest. Gadwalls usually fly in small compact flocks and are fast fliers with very rapid

Gadwall.

wingbeats. The drakes whistle, and both sexes quack like mallards but with a somewhat softer, lower tone.

WIDGEON

This duck is sometimes also called the baldpate. An easy identifying field mark on both sexes is a white belly and forewing; the speculum is black and metallic green. The male has a white crown with a dark mask. Easily alarmed and quick to fly, the widgeon moves in a fast twisting and turning motion. It often feeds with divers, robbing them of food they

Widgeon.

bring up from the bottom. The drakes whistle; the hens make a soft quack.

BLACK DUCK

The black duck is found mostly in Eastern (Atlantic and Mississippi) flyways. It is the wariest duck and one of the most challenging to hunt. Larger rivers are its primary habitat. Both sexes are a dark chocolate brown with lighter, mottled brown heads. The grayish white underwing, which shows in flight, is an identifying mark. The male's bill and feet are

Black Duck.

brighter than the female's. The black duck flies in V's or lines and sometimes in flocks. The call is like the mallard's. Black ducks make large and very tasty table birds.

GOLDEN-EYE

Golden-eyes are easily identified by the whistle of their wings in flight, which is clearly heard from some distance. For this reason they are also called whistlers. Golden-eyes are found on both coasts. They are identified in flight by distinctive patterns of black and white. The female has a brown head and gray body; the male has a large head, sometimes tinged

Golden-eye.

with green, and a white cheek patch. They tend to rise from water in a fast, spiraling takeoff. The drakes make a piercing high-pitched call; the hens quack.

CANVASBACK

The canvasback is an extremely strong and fast flier, beating its wings quickly and noisily. Although the canvasback appears very similar to the scaup and redhead on water, it can easily be distinguished by the slope of its forehead. "Cans" usually fly in V-flocks or long waving lines. The drakes make a croaking sound, and the hens produce a quack similar to that of mallards. To many waterfowlers the canvasback is one of the tastiest birds. Its large size also makes this duck well worth the extra effort it sometimes requires to collect. "Cans" are extremely wary and hardy bay and sea ducks. They require the utmost in blind preparation

Canvasback.

and decoy sets, as well as an affinity for rough water—for you will probably get thoroughly soaked before a limit is filled.

REDHEAD

Often traveling with the canvasbacks, this larger bird is a bit grayer than
the "Can" and has a bluish bill. The male has a red head, black breast,
and gray body; the hen is brown, with gray wings. Redheads are found
from coast to coast. They fly in large V-flocks, but are sometimes found in
irregular formations while in feeding areas. They make fast movements in
flight and often raft in large flocks in deep water, then move out in the
morning and evening to feed in shallow water. The drakes make a low,
rasping sound; the hens quack with a sound higher than that of the
mallard hen.

Redhead.

Black Scoter.

BLACK SCOTER

A sea duck, the black scoter is the smallest of the scoters; it is sometimes called the common scoter. The male is entirely black, with an orange swelling around the base of the bill; the female is dark brown, with a light gray face and throat. Scoters normally appear all black at a distance. They are birds of the open icy seas and are mostly found in the far north of Alaska and Canada. They usually fly in a long, strung-out line and are silent.

SURF SCOTER

Surf scoters are large diving ducks. The most agile of the scoters, they fly swiftly but seldom in the follow-the-leader style of the other scoters. The

Surf Scoter.

male is mostly black, with white patches on the top and forehead; the female is dark brown, with light patches on both sides of the eyes. Surf scoters are primarily found in the open seas of Alaska and other Northern regions. They are usually silent.

WHITE-WINGED SCOTER

This scoter is a deep water or "sea" diver, the largest of the scoters. The male is dusky black, with white wing patches and a white crescent around the eyes; the female is more drab. The birds are found primarily in New England, where they are sometimes called coots. An old-fashioned "coot shoot" was one way of hunting these ducks—hunters would watch the ducks' travel pattern, then simply row over and start shooting.

White-winged Scoter.

The long wavering lines of coots did not vary from their flight, but just kept coming through the gunfire. The white-winged scoter often ventures inland. The ducks sit on the water in tight rafts and fly in long, strung-out lines. For the most part they are silent.

SCAUP

Scaups are also called "bluebills" or "broadbills." The male is dark on each end and white in the middle; the hen is an even brown, with a lighter strip on the wings. The best identifying mark for this bird is a

Scaup.

♂

♀

light strip on the wings, about half the wing length on the lesser scaup and two-thirds on the greater scaup. Scaups fly in fast, compact flocks, usually fairly low. Their wings produce a loud rustling sound. They tend to raft on large bodies of water during the day and are very restless while on the water. Scaup drakes make a "b-r-r-r-r-r" sound; the hens are usually silent.

HARLEQUIN DUCK

This medium-sized duck has an Eastern and a Western population. The drake is a beautiful slate blue with brown sides, and has an easily recognizable pattern of white spots and strips edged with black on the head, neck, and chest. The hen is smaller and doesn't have the distinctive white patches on its wings and chest; however, its head is spotted. Harlequin ducks sometimes appear along mountain streams, but they are generally

♂

Harlequin Duck.

♀

coastal. They are usually by themselves, but at times will swim with scoters. They swim with a bobbing motion of their long tails and are almost always silent.

OLDSQUAW

Found on both coasts, this "deep diver" is easily identified by the bold black, white, and brown pattern of its winter plumage and the long, pointed central tail feather. The female is somewhat smaller and less spectacular in color and lacks the tail feather. It is the only diving duck that is light in back and dark in front. Oldsquaws are found in loose rafts

Oldsquaw.

on large inland lakes and along the coasts, as well as on the open sea. They are fast fliers and move mostly at night. Oldsquaws are very vocal, giving off a sharp, piercing whistle.

BUFFLEHEAD

Buffleheads are the smallest of the diving ducks. They fly in very small flocks, low over the water, and with fast wingbeats. In flight the hen appears dark gray and the drake black and white. The drake is easily recognized by its large puffy head and black and white pattern. The

Bufflehead.

white extends back from the eyes and the body is black and white. These beautiful little ducks are usually late migrators. Buffleheads are normally silent, but sometimes they make soft quacks.

RUDDY DUCK

The ruddy duck is a small diver that will often disappear under the water rather than fly when disturbed. The drake is a deep brown, and has a black head with a white cheek patch and a blue bill; the hen is mostly gray, with a cheek patch divided by a brown bar. These unusual ducks are easy to spot on the water because the fanlike tail of both sexes is held erect while the duck swims. Ruddy ducks seem to have a hard time getting off the water and fly unevenly and noisily. They are usually silent.

Ruddy Duck.

GEESE

CANADA GOOSE

A primary target for many waterfowlers, these easily recognized birds have a white cheek patch, a black bill, and a black neck. The rest of the body is colored in subtle shades of gray; and the belly near the tail is white. Almost every state is trying to build and establish populations of this fine game bird. At one time its populations were very low, but as a result of excellent management, far-sighted regulations, and an adaptability to today's land use, the Canada goose is now back in bigger numbers than ever. A great deal of the credit for this goes to dedicated hunters

Canada Goose.

who not only carefully follow gamebag limits and the highly restricted type of hunting needed these past few years, but also give help through their donations to various federal, state, and local programs that work to restore these stately birds. There are eleven known subspecies, ranging from the Giant Canada, which may weigh as much as 16 pounds, to the tiny Cackling Canada, which is not much larger than a mallard. The call of the Canada goose is the well-known "kerrrr-onk!" A complete gabble of voices makes quite a din when the earth and sky are filled with milling geese.

SNOW GOOSE

The largest goose after the Canada, the snow goose is pure white except for its black wingtips. It has a grayish pink bill and feet. Snow geese are not quite as trusting as Canada geese and offer a much more challenging

Snow Goose.

hunt. They have a tendency to migrate in huge flocks, so that they are very abundant in circumscribed areas as they move through the country. There are two subspecies of snow goose, the greater snow goose and the lesser snow goose. The latter is much more abundant, being almost as plentiful as the Canada goose. The call of the snow goose is far higher than that of the Canada; most hunters who go after this particular goose use a call made especially shrill, or whittle down the reed of their goose call to make it higher pitched.

BLUE GOOSE

The blue goose is actually a color phase of the lesser snow goose. It has the white head, pink legs and feet of the snow goose, but its body is a slate gray color. Many times lesser snow geese and blues will be in the

Blue Goose.

same flock. The blue goose weighs from 6 to 7 pounds, as does the lesser snow. Its call is a muffled, higher-pitched version of the Canada goose call.

WHITE-FRONTED GOOSE (SPECKLEBELLY)

Resembling the Canada goose in size, coloring, and flight formation, the white-fronted goose is one of the most widely distributed, and is a favorite in California as well as along the Platte River in Nebraska. The white-fronted goose has about the same coloring as the Canada, except that the white patch on the cheek of the Canada appears on the forehead of the white-fronted goose. Another distinguishing mark is the dark streaks or "speckles" on the upper belly, giving the goose the nickname of "Speckle-

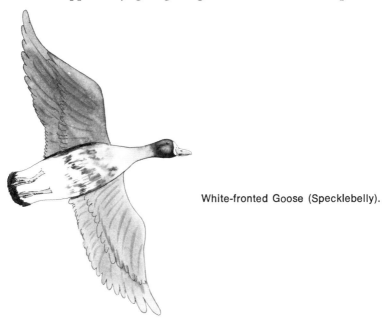

White-fronted Goose (Specklebelly).

belly." The bill is pink with a touch of blue, and the legs are a bright yellow. Specklebellies are frequently mixed in flocks of snows and blues. They weigh from 4 to 8 pounds. Often called the "laughing goose," the white fronts make a rapid series of high, hysterical laughing sounds. They are very hard to call.

BRANT

Brants are small, dark geese. They have shorter necks and lack the cheek patch of the Canada, and they have a white neck mark. The Black Brant

Brant.

is a western goose very similar to the regular Brant except that it has a darker belly. Their flight is fast and low over the water, usually in a strung-out line. At one time Brants were very rare, but they are now making a comeback. Both sexes make a soft "cooonnk" sound.

OTHER WATERFOWL

COMMON MERGANSER

The merganser is an extremely strong and fast flier, often moving in a strung-out, follow-the-leader style low over the water. The drakes show a lot of white in flight; the hens appear dark gray. Mergansers winter in the North as well as in the coastal waters of the Southern states. Their only sound is a low, rasping "croak."

Common Merganser.

AMERICAN COOT

Although disdained by some waterfowlers because of its eating habits, to others this small bird offers some sport, mostly because of the high bag limits. Both male and female are dusky black, with a white bill and white patch. Coots inhabit many large, man-made impoundments all over the country, and winter in the North. Their call is a short, low rasping sound.

American Coot.

♂

♀

4

Calling for Ducks and Geese

A wavering cluster of tiny black spots is sighted in the distant sunrise, and everyone in the reed-covered blind unconsciously tenses as the caller puts the hand-worn walnut call to his lips. From deep inside him comes a harsh, guttural grunt which ends in a clear-ringing, confident sound. Again he gives the call and is joined by another hunter in the blind. Suddenly the flight of ducks turns and heads directly for the blind and its set of carefully placed decoys. The caller abruptly changes his sound and softens his tone as the fast-flying ducks draw closer and closer. No one moves a muscle as the flight comes in high, necks outstretched and weaving, cautious eyes examining every particle of the scene below them. The caller is alone again, this time gently clucking and begging the flight. The sound is contented, confident. With whistling wings the sunrise-flecked birds sweep past the left side of the blind, and the caller barks a high, fast call, then quickly slides down to his clucking and grunting. No one moves as the ducks appear to the right of the blind, completing a slow circle. The caller continues to cluck ever so softly; he's not begging now. Seconds pass like hours as the ducks begin to lose altitude and "lock up" for their splashy landing. They're close now, so close it's easy to distinguish drakes from hens, even in the dim light. Big red feet outstretched, they slowly drop to the water, less than 24 yards from the three hunters crouched in the cold blind. "Now," breathes the caller, and the hunters quickly rise and fire at their chosen birds. After the noise and confusion, three mallard drakes bob in the disturbed water, and an eager Labrador is released to start his day's work.

Calling ducks into decoys is not a mysterious, secret talent that can be practiced only by a select few. Successful duck calling is a skill that can be learned just as easily as learning to shoot a gun or use a fishing rod. Mastering proper calling does take a great deal of practice, however, and a sensitive ear that can determine the nuances in the call and control it for the proper sound.

The most widely hunted species of duck is the mallard, and the techniques given below are basically for calling mallards. If you learn to call mallards properly, you can use the same calls to attract almost all other puddle or "dabbler" ducks.

The duck-calling methods illustrated here are written by professional "callers" and are based on years of observing, listening to, and "talking to" ducks in marshes and fields. Duck-calling methods vary a great deal, but the techniques given have been tested and proven time and again not only by professional guides in the fields but in competitions such as the World Duck Calling Contest. When you become an accomplished caller, you will not only find duck hunting increasingly thrilling, but will also

"First-year caller"—and the results of his efforts.

LEARNING DUCK LANGUAGE

Like learning any language, long hours of listening are required to become "fluent." If you can't make your own tapes, kits like these can help.

By taping and then listening to ducks "talking" at a local pond or refuge, you can practice and perfect your calls.

become a better and more selective hunter. A good caller does not have to resort to "sky-busting," nor does he have to take any chances on crippling ducks or mistakenly taking protected species as a result of long-range shooting. A good caller can literally bring ducks into his "lap" and then select his shots with no fear that he will cripple a distant target. You'll know you have become a "master caller" when you're able to call ducks into your decoys, allow them to land, and then continue to "talk their language" without scaring them off.

You can't learn to call ducks without hearing for yourself how the different duck calls sound. There are basically two ways of doing this. If you're lucky enough to live close to a waterfowl refuge or even a city park with a duck pond, you can listen and talk to ducks in these areas. Tape a bit of duck talk with a cartridge tape cassette, then listen to it at your leisure. Or you can buy one of the many duck-calling records on the market and study it. One excellent way of learning duck calls is to record actual duck talk or the calls from records onto a cassette, then play the tape in your car on your way to work. Practice along with the cassette until you sound just like the duck.

If you've ever gone jump shooting for ducks, you know there is one call that should never be used, and that is the alarm call made when ducks are surprised or scared off while on the water. This call starts low and slides up quickly to an extremely high note.

CALLING MALLARD DUCKS

Holding the Call

The first thing to learn is the correct way of holding the call. Grip the call between the thumb and forefinger. If you are a left-handed shooter, you should learn to call with your right hand. If you are right-handed, call with your left. Of course, it's not a bad idea to be able to call with either hand, for there may be times when this will come in very useful.

With the call gripped properly by thumb and forefingers, cup your fingers and close them. Opening and closing your fingers as you use the call can add variety to your tones and give more realism to the sounds.

Placing the Call in the Mouth

It is very important that the call is placed in the mouth properly, because you must be able to trap all the air. Air escaping around the call will make it hard to blow.

HOW TO GRIP THE CALL

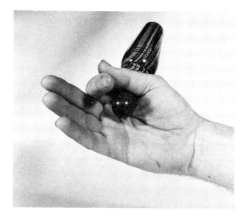

First, cradle the call loosely between your thumb and forefinger.

Then, to add variety and realism to your clucks and feeding chatter, open and close your hand.

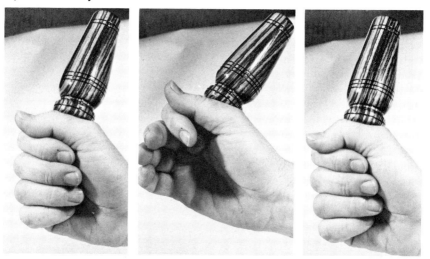

Place the call inside your bottom lip and press your top lip against it just hard enough to prevent air from escaping around the call.

Grunting Into the Call

Contrary to popular belief, you do not blow into a call; you "grunt" into it, and that's the hardest part for any beginner. The air must be forced into the call from deep in your chest, rolling or forcing your diaphragm up to give the deep guttural sound. Merely blowing into the

PLACING THE CALL

Correct mouth placement is also important. Position the call on the inside of your bottom lip, then bring it up against your upper lip. Keep the lips tight to prevent air from escaping around the call.

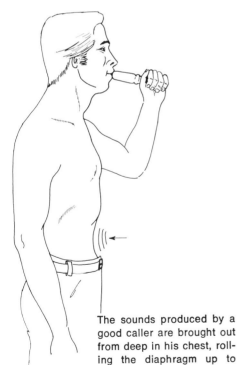

The sounds produced by a good caller are brought out from deep in his chest, rolling the diaphragm up to force a "grunt" or large volume of air through the call.

call produces a hollow, high-pitched sound which not only sounds fake but also doesn't carry very far. The illustration shows the muscles that must be used to force air into the call.

Words Used in Calling

When you grunt into the call, you must actually say or form one of three words with which you can achieve almost every kind of puddle duck call. The three words are WICK, TICK-IT, and KAK.

WICK

Pronouncing the word WICK and at the same time grunting into the call produces the most important call—*the quack of the hen mallard.* Practice this word on your call until you can give a perfect hen mallard quack. Stretching the word out like this gives it a little more realistic sound:

    WI-CK   WI-CK   WI-CK   WI-CK

Now learn to do this five or six times without stopping.

    WI-CK   WI-CK   WI-CK   WI-CK   WI-CK   WI-CK

The call should sound like the soft "quack, quack, quack, quack, quack, quack" of a lone hen mallard. Once you have mastered this call, go on to the next.

TICK-IT

The word TICK-IT is the feed chatter of puddle ducks and is pronounced into the call. At the same time move your tongue up and down, bouncing it off the roof of your mouth. Say the word TICK-IT slowly, then gradually speed up until you are saying it as fast as you can. It will sound like this:

    TICK-IT   TICK-IT   TICK-IT   TICK-IT   TICK-IT

    TICK-IT-TICK-IT-TICK-IT-TICK-IT-TICK-IT-TICK-IT-TICK-IT

Don't become discouraged. This call takes lots of practice, but it is extremely effective when a flight of ducks is warily circling your blind. In fact, if a caller could learn only one call, the feed chatter would be the most important.

KAK

When grunted into the call, the word KAK produces *the cluck of the hen mallard,* which you can mix in with the feed chatter to gain a variety of sounds.

    KAK   KAK   KAK   KAK   KAK   KAK   KAK

    KAK   KAK   KAK   KAK   KAK   KAK   KAK   KAK   KAK

Learn to stagger this call between the TICK-IT feed chatter, and you have mastered the feeding sounds of a contented mallard.

The Hail Call or Highball Call

Use only one word in this call, WICK. Pronounced into the call, it produces the quack the hen mallard gives to attract ducks flying some distance away.

Pronounce WICK as loud as you can, forcing the sound until you "break" on a high note. Now hold this high sound for the count of five, like this:

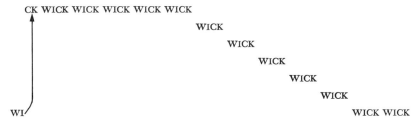

When you can hit this high note and hold it, go up to it and pronounce the word WICK five times, then come down the scale as fast as you can until you run out of air. Practice this until you can do it with ease. It's hard to learn, but it will come to you all at once and sound like this:

```
CK WICK WICK WICK WICK WICK
 |                         WICK
 |                              WICK
 |                                   WICK
 |                                        WICK
 |                                             WICK
WI/                                               WICK WICK
```

You can use this call when ducks are 150 to 1,000 yards away or when you see high-flying flocks overhead. It is most effective with two or more hunters staggering the calls to produce a barrage of sound. On foggy, overcast mornings, if you give this call over and over again, it will attract ducks that you cannot see.

The Close-in Hail Call

When the ducks are about 100 yards or closer, switch to a *close-in hail call*—also called the *five quack* or *landing call*. It starts fairly high and comes down fast:

```
WICK
     WICK
          WICK
               WICK
                    WICK
```

If ducks are circling or are out about 100 yards, give the close-in hail call very fast. When the flock starts toward you, go into a feed chatter until the ducks land in the decoys or fly into shooting range. When calling conditions are rough (on public hunting land, for example), give the close-in hail call over and over again until you attract attention from passing ducks. If the ducks start in and then turn away, give a *comeback call*.

The Comeback Call

You use only one word in this call, WICK:

WICK   WICK   WICK
           WICK
          WICK
           WICK
                WICK   WICK   WICK   WICK

The comeback call also starts fairly high, comes down fast, and ends with a stretched-out, begging sound.

Use this call when ducks are trying to land just outside your decoys. If ducks are going away from you, keep blowing this call over and over until they turn back toward you, but leave out the begging part until they turn. Try to be demanding on the first part of the comeback call, but beg just a little on the end. When the ducks turn and start back toward you, go into the next call, which is the *close-in call*.

The Close-in Call

You use only the word WICK in this call. Drag it out as you say it:

WI - - - - - - - - CK   WI - - - - - - - - CK   WI - - - - - - - - CK   WI - - - - - - - - CK

Pronounce the word WICK with a slow, dragging sound like this, coming down the scale as you do so:

WI - - - - - - CK
       WI - - - - - - CK
           WI - - - - - - CK
               WI - - - - - - CK
                   WI - - - - - CK

Give this call four or five times, then mix it with feed chatter when the ducks are circling your decoys or are out about 60 yards and coming toward you. Then when the ducks are getting close, go into the feed chatter only.

The Lonesome Hen or Mating Call

Two words are used in this call, WICK and KAK. This makes the cluck of the hen mallard:

```
WICK          WICK          WICK
KAK    KAK    KAK    KAK    KAK    KAK
KAK KAK KAK KAK KAK KAK KAK
WICK
     WICK
          WICK
               WICK
                    WICK - - - - - - - - - - - WI - - - - - - - - - - CK
```

This call used with the feed chatter is very effective on single drakes or small flocks. Repeat it two or three times without stopping.

CALLING TEAL, WIDGEON, PINTAIL, AND DIVING DUCKS

There are certain different techniques and calls that attract teal, widgeon, pintails, and especially diving ducks.

Teal

Even though teal are relatively easy to call using mallard-calling techniques, the calls they give are made up of peeps, whistles, twitters, and very fast, faint quacks. Sometimes using a commercial pintail whistle or even a common toy police whistle along with your duck call will bring them in when working with a mallard call alone isn't doing the trick. Needless to say, you should use the whistling and peeping sounds sparingly and faintly. It's a good idea to have one caller in the blind using the whistle while another simulates the faint fast quacking of the teal using a regular mallard call. The idea is to mix the sounds together.

Widgeon and Pintail

Mixing whistles with mallard calls will also bring in widgeons and pintails more readily. If you are in a principal pintail flyway, use mostly pintail decoys with a few mallards mixed in with the set. By using a commercial pintail call or, again, a toy whistle along with your mallard call, you'll have greater success. As in teal calling, these calls are done best with two or more callers staggering their calls. Call softly and not too often when whistling.

Diving Ducks

Most of the calls made by diving ducks consist of purrs and soft meows, although they sometimes produce sharp, barklike calls. A canvas-

TIMING DUCK CALLS

The hail call is blown when ducks are about 100 yards out.

When the ducks start to circle your blind at about 60 yards, give the close-in call.

If they turn and start away, give the come-back call.

The feed chatter is used when flocks are close but don't know whether to come on in. It is also very effective on single drakes and small flocks.

back or a redhead hen's quack is similar to that of a mallard hen, but the sound is usually a little higher pitched.

Fluttering your tongue against the roof of your mouth and at the same time grunting into your duck call will produce a "Buuuuuu-RRRRRRR" sound which simulates the purring made by divers. Using the word WICK, pronounced very fast and with a sharp grunt, will produce the barklike sound. You can also give the word WICK when making the quacking sounds of divers, but a little higher pitched than when calling mallards. Usually a few high quacks will get their attention. Then start with the purrs and meows and you'll be bringing divers flocking into your spread. Just remember—divers are not as talkative and noisy as puddle ducks, whether in flight or feeding.

Poor calling can scare off more ducks than you could attract with a thousand decoys, so learn to call properly. Then do it with confidence.

CALLING GEESE

Successfully calling geese into your decoys is as satisfying and challenging as calling ducks. To many waterfowlers, pulling a flight of wary big old honkers within shooting range is a lifetime dream.

Calling geese is in many ways similar to calling ducks. The calls are a little larger and shaped differently, but they are held in the hand and positioned against the lips in exactly the same way. The call is always blown through the large end, your lips completely covering the edge of the mouthpiece so as to prevent air from escaping around your lips.

The calls of the Canadian goose can be used to attract most smaller

Typical goose call.

geese as well, although the calls for the smaller geese should be sharper and quicker. Many expert callers like to have two goose calls with them, one that is high and sharp for snows and blues, and one with a deeper, more resonant tone for the Canadian honkers. Another way of producing this tone for Canadian geese is to pull the end of the call down against your chest and cup your hands against it. If done correctly, you won't muffle the sound yet will produce a deep, resonant tone.

To achieve proper control and the deep sounds needed, you must also learn to "grunt" into the goose call just as you do in using a duck call. Grunting out the sound rather than merely blowing into the calls is the secret of any good calling, yet it is the hardest to learn. It's like learning how to ride a bicycle or swim; at first it seems almost impossible, then all of a sudden you can do it.

The best way to learn the calls is to go to a waterfowl refuge and listen to goose talk. Try to determine what the sounds are and then imitate them. Again, you can also learn a great deal by listening to professional callers on tapes or records, but you're getting it second hand. Learn it directly and you'll be pulling in flights of geese to your decoys regularly.

Calling in geese requires a lot of "gabble."

Greeting Call

The first goose call to learn is the *greeting call*, which should be blown when a ragged V of geese starts coming toward your blind or passes over your area. The greeting is a two-note call, consisting of a low first sound, "ker," and a high-pitched sound, "honk." To make these two notes, first blow with just enough force into the call to produce the low sound. Then, without stopping your force of air, increase the air pressure with a sharp intake of your stomach, forcing the call to change to the higher note. The call should sound like "kerahh—onk."

Make sure there is no break between the two notes, and that you do not let the air pressure drop low enough to allow the last of the yelp to fall back to the low note. Some callers like to make two or three high yelps before dropping to the lower guttural sound. This call should be given fairly rapidly as the geese come toward you. It helps to have more than one caller in the blind, each trying to out-honk the other, as geese on the ground do.

When the geese get within 100 yards, call about once every 3 to 6 seconds. If the birds honk back, increase the frequency of your calling; if they start to veer away from your decoy spread, call just a little faster.

The Feed Call

When the geese start moving in closer to the blind and working your decoys, switch to the feeding call. This is produced by a series of short grunts made into your call. The grunts should be light enough to keep the call in the lower register and close together; the sound is similar to the first part of the greeting call, but lower and much softer. You can pull the call against you chest and cup your hands against it to produce the muted feeding gabble.

When the geese start to set their wings and close in, don't do anything. Don't call, don't move a muscle, don't even blink an eyelash. Soon you'll collect a trophy that would make any waterfowler happy.

MAINTAINING AND CLEANING DUCK AND GOOSE CALLS

Duck and goose calls are made with two types of reeds, either metal (usually brass or bronze) or plastic. Today, most calls are manufactured with plastic reeds, although some professional callers still use metal reeds. Plastic reed calls are much easier to blow and easier for the manufacturer to make. However, they will occasionally stick up or stick together when full of saliva.

When you are doing a lot of calling in cold weather, remember to wipe the moisture from inside the barrel of your call from time to time. Also, wear the call on a lanyard and keep it inside your coat pocket when not using it to reduce sticking problems in freezing weather. Professional

GOOSE CALLS

A greeting call is used to attract a flight of geese.

Then the feed call is used as they turn and head in toward you.

To produce the feed call, you should hold your head down and pull the call against your chest, muffling the sound and lowering it.

Learn to take apart your call, remove any obstruction, and put it back together again properly tuned.

Always wear your call on a lanyard so it won't drop into the mud in the blind. Keep the call close to your body to prevent the reed from freezing and sticking.

callers always have an extra call handy which they can grab if their usual call gets stuck at just the wrong moment.

All duck calls are constructed basically the same way; you should know how to disassemble your calls, clean them, and put them back together properly tuned.

To clean a call, simply remove the mouthpiece from the sound pipe, then remove the reed holder. Without the reed holder, the reed can easily be withdrawn and all the components thoroughly cleaned by wiping or blowing foreign matter and water away. If necessary, a new reed can be placed in the call.

To reassemble the call, place the reed on the surface of the mouthpiece and insert it as far back into the mouthpiece as it will go. This sets the reed in the proper position on most calls. If your call is a good one, it will be tuned exactly as it was when you purchased it.

Repairing Calls

If you do a lot of calling during the season, the reed should be replaced. If the reed holder is a cork one, it should also be replaced at least every six months. A tight cork or reed holder is very important to the quality of your call's sound.

Tuning Your Call

Tuning most calls is simple and fast. It can be done right in your blind or in the field if necessary. Place the reed in the call as far back in the mouthpiece as possible. Place the reed holder in position. Blow. If your call is too low pitched, cut about $\frac{1}{64}$th of an inch off the end of the reed with a sharp knife or a pair of scissors. Blow the call again. Keep cutting off the reed until you achieve the tone you want. Be sure to blow the call every time you cut the reed off.

If the call is too high pitched, the reed is too short, and you'll need a new reed blank. Do not pull a reed out of position in the mouthpiece to achieve a lower tone. If you do this, it becomes very difficult to replace the reed in the exact position should it require retuning later. Once you have cut the reed to achieve the tone you desire, cut extra reeds to the same length, and they will be tuned when placed in the call. You might want to cut both a lower-pitched and a higher-pitched reed to carry for special occasions.

You should always carry a couple of extra "pre-tuned" reeds on a hunting trip. You may lose a reed while cleaning out the call, you may break one if the weather is freezing, or you might want a higher- or lower-pitched reed as an extra.

DUCK-CALLING CONTESTS

Most states have a duck-calling contest every year sponsored by a Ducks Unlimited chapter or other sporting organization. The winners of the state contests are eligible to call in the World Champion Duck Calling Contest held in Stuttgart, Arkansas, every December.

The rules of these contests are fairly standard. You call for 1 minute and 30 seconds, demonstrating the following calls:

Hail Call
Comeback Call
Feed Chatter
Lonesome Hen or Mating Call

These contests are a lot of fun, and as an entrant you will be competing with some of the best duck callers and hunters in the country.

ADJUSTMENT AND MAINTENANCE OF CALLS

To replace a call reed, you need scissors or a knife, a reed blank, an extra reed holder, and an ignition file (or you can use your fingernail).

The first step in replacing a new reed is to set the reed in position as far into the call as possible, then push it into the reed holder.

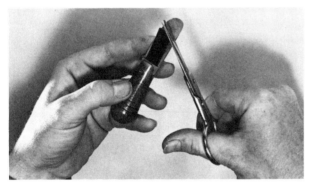

Clip off the corners and end of the reed until you achieve the sound you desire. Reassemble the call and blow on it after each piece is cut off.

To fine-tune the call, use a fine file and just barely cut material off the end of the new reed.

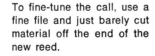

♀

♂

5

Decoys

The drama of watching a flight of red-leg mallards warily circle, then finally settle into your hand-carved and painted decoys, and the lung-bursting effort of trying to hold absolutely still while a half dozen jumbo-jet-sized geese glide down slowly and gently among 100 plywood silhouettes on the frosty ground, are experiences no waterfowler can forget. Decoying ducks and geese is waterfowling at its best, providing the hunter with close-up hunting that just can't be beaten.

American Indians used rush and reed decoys to bring mallards and other puddle ducks within bow-and-arrow range long before white men arrived in North America. Hand-carved wooden decoys are a product of American artistry that is just beginning to be recognized, and an old decoy carved by a master like Shang Wheeler can bring an extremely high price. Back in the 1800s decoy making was at its height, and market hunters who shot geese and ducks for profit gunned with as many as 600 or 700 decoys.

Today's gunning is an entirely different story, but good decoys are even more important than they were a century ago. Today's waterfowl

Decoy-making is an art dating back to early nineteenth-century America; these antique hand-carved blocks are still providing plenty of gunning action.

are much smarter and more wary, and it takes a real good stool of decoys to fool a big flight of mallards or "Cans."

DECOYING DUCKS

Many modern decoys are factory-made, not handcrafted, and come in several different styles. Most are made from some sort of plastic. Some decoys are hollow, made of solid plastic; others are solid and made of foam plastic. Some again are made of heavy rubber, and inflate when they are thrown into the water. The most popular are made of flexible but hard-molded plastic, and are not only realistically shaped but have the finest feather markings molded in.

There are hundreds of decoy sets—one for every kind of hunting. Each set you make will be different from any other, and its deployment will be governed by terrain, weather, how the birds are flying, and many other factors. After several years of hunting experience, the gunner begins to read all these details and can put out consistently successful sets. But there are certain guidelines that help make a set of blocks produce.

Decoying Puddle Ducks

The most easily decoyed ducks are mallards; and yet at times they can be downright stubborn, with flight after flight turning down your best offers. Almost all other puddle ducks and even some divers will decoy to mallard sets, though there are decoys made for most every species.

Setting out "dekes" is the first morning chore.

Early in the year when the teal start migrating, many shooters like to put out a small teal spread for this fast-moving little duck, but gunners will often add an occasional mallard to give the teal more confidence. These early season decoys should be smeared a bit with mud and allowed to dry. This will dull the bright colors and make the decoys appear more lifelike. Early in the season, most ducks have not yet developed their full plumage and appear somewhat drab. Male and female puddle ducks can be mixed in the sets, though with more females than males.

As the season progresses and the ducks become more wary, a few pintails mixed in with a set of mallards will help make the late season ducks decoy more easily. Some gunners like to put other confidence decoys in their sets, like a couple of Canada geese feeding on the shoreline next to the blind, or a group of coots, seagulls, or even a hand-carved wooden blue heron. However, these decoys should not be mixed in with a spread of mallards or puddle ducks, but placed somewhere off to the side.

Place the majority of your decoys upwind of the blind, and leave an

MALLARD AND PINTAIL DECOYS

Typical plastic mallard (left) and pintail (right) decoys.

Handmade cork mallard decoy.

open space in front of it. Mallards like to come in against the wind, and they will often pass over a few ducks to land in the opening by your main set. Place a few decoys on the outside edge of this opening about 40 yards away from your blind. In this way you'll know when the ducks are within shooting range.

Keep the majority of your decoys away from the shoreline and vegetation. Most ducks don't like to get too near the shore because of the danger of predators. Furthermore, it's harder for the incoming ducks to spot the decoys.

In normal shooting, decoys should be well spread out, with groups fairly close together, about 2 to 8 feet apart. In cold weather, however, ducks will huddle closer to help keep the water open and to stay warm. Some hunters tell you never to set duck decoys close together because they look like birds that are about to flush; but when it's cold, the closer the better. A tight spread of decoys would be about 1 to 2 feet apart.

Wind direction doesn't make any difference in attracting ducks, but it should be taken into consideration to give you the best shooting positions.

Never let anyone hurry you when setting out your decoys, even if flights are starting to pass overhead. A well-placed set is much more valuable than a bunch of decoys thoughtlessly tossed into the water.

A little breeze is good for decoying because the decoys will move and shift slightly with the wind. On windless days, when birds seem to shy from your set, you might try making up a feeder or swimming duck. The feeding duck is merely a decoy anchored at the edge of your set well out in the open part of the water. A line is tied to the front of the decoy and threaded through a heavy anchor on the bottom. This line is brought back to the blind, and when ducks are overhead and warily circling, the line is pulled to make the feeder tip under water. Releasing the line will make it pop back up in a lifelike way. A swimming duck is made in much

Feeding and swimming decoys are easy to make yet they are very effective in attracting ducks into a set. Both decoys only require a simple anchor and some string.

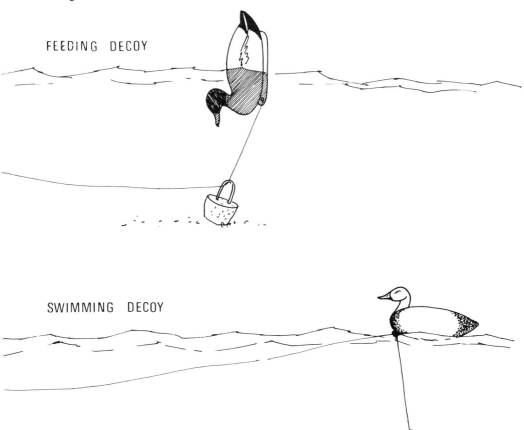

FEEDING DECOY

SWIMMING DECOY

the same way. A length of line is run some distance out to an anchor on the bottom of the duck lake. The line is run through an eye on the anchor, and the ends are brought back to the blind and tied together. A decoy is tied to the line: by pulling it back and forth through the water, you can make the decoy swim through the stool realistically.

To make a good-looking set, the heads of the ducks must be in various positions, some turned back for sleep, some tipping for food, some turned right and some left. One position that should not be over-done is the outstretched neck. This is the danger position and means the flock has spotted trouble and is ready for flight. If you have ever watched a flock of contented resting ducks, you will remember that most of them had their heads tucked well down on their chests. This is the attitude you want in most of your decoys.

POTHOLE SETS

The most common decoy spread is the pothole set used in small marsh openings, ponds, and potholes. The best system for setting up decoys in a pothole or small slough is to scatter them around the edge of the water, leaving an opening in the center and in front of the blind. Puddle ducks have more control in landing than divers and will normally land in smaller openings.

A good set for most small waters would be a couple of dozen mallard decoys, two or three pintails, and two or three widgeon.

Other good pothole patterns include a string of decoys to the left or right of your blind (depending on the direction of the wind), or two groups, on either side of the blind, with an opening in the middle.

FIELD SETS

Field shooting for mallards can be extremely exciting. The best method is to group the decoys around the blind, with the majority located in the front. Again, leave an opening in the middle of the set and in front of the blind for the ducks to land in. If you plan to do much field shooting for mallards, you would be wise to invest in the oversize magnum decoys, because they're easier for ducks to spot over the stubble of grain and from the high altitude from which they work a grain field.

TIMBER SETS

In timber shooting you can disregard almost all decoy set rules. Merely find a good opening in the flooded timber, place about a half dozen decoys in the opening, step behind the next tree, and wait for the ducks to funnel in—for funnel in they will!

COMBINATION SETS

In many large freshwater lakes the waterfowler can gun for both puddle and diver ducks. A combination rig, if used the right way, can provide some great gunning; but if you're using both divers and puddle duck decoys, keep the two separate. Place the divers in the deep open water and the puddlers near shore. It's not a bad idea to place a half dozen broadbills quite near your puddle duck rig.

DIVER SETS

Shooting divers over shore blinds is similar to shooting puddle ducks. However, in rigging stake blinds, boat blinds, layouts, or sneakboats, the patterns are somewhat different. In this case the idea is to help break up the profile of the blind with the decoys. Group some of the decoys tightly around the boat or blind, with a large opening directly in front of it. Most large rigs should have about the same number of hens and drakes. There is usually a larger group of ducks setting somewhat tighter than the rest.

One of the traditional systems for open water sets is the fish hook, called the "pipe" set by old-timers. In this system the main body of decoys is set near your blind, and a string of decoys is run out into the open water to attract distant flying waterfowl. These sets are normally quite large, consisting of several hundred decoys; they are extremely effective on both large inland lakes and open water. The number of decoys varies with the size of the body of water.

You can mix magnums or oversize decoys with normal-sized decoys in these spreads because in a real flock there will be both large and small birds. Use the larger birds on the outside and in the lead line so they will be spotted more easily from a distance. You can also use goose decoys for this lead to bring birds in out of open water.

After they have been gunned, divers have a tendency to avoid flying over land if they can help it; therefore, you should place your decoys so the birds can approach them over water.

When putting out large numbers of decoys, you can tie two to an anchor or even place them on a cross-board the way market hunters did when they put out several hundred decoys for a morning shoot.

Because their short wings give them less control, divers need lots of room to land, and they will often fly over a stool to land past the decoys. When the water gets rough, bunch your decoys closer; they'll show up better as they move up and down in the troughs. If storms are brewing, place your decoys on the more protected side of the points of land and islands. Ducks will be looking for these sheltered spots.

COMMON PUDDLE DUCK DECOY SETS

Puddle ducks are found in many different kinds of areas. Each location requires its own type of set to attract the ducks and insure a good day's shooting.

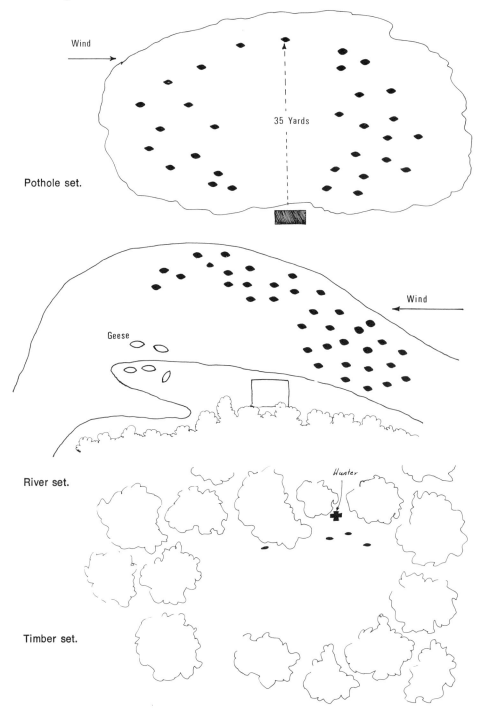

Wind

35 Yards

Pothole set.

Wind

Geese

River set.

Hunter

Timber set.

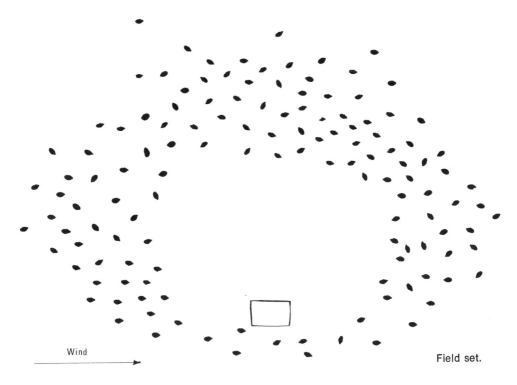

Wind →

Field set.

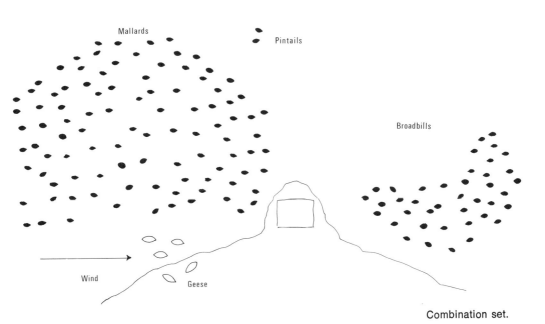

Mallards

Pintails

Broadbills

Wind →

Geese

Combination set.

One good way of creating a more realistic set is to use ducks that have been shot, bracing their heads in a natural position with a forked branch pushed into the marsh mud.

Typical manufactured diver ducks, scaup and redhead.

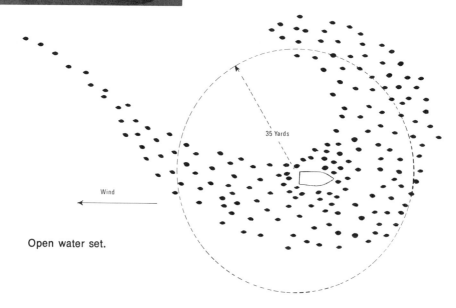

35 Yards

Wind

Open water set.

DECOYING GEESE

Decoys Over Land

A set of decoys for bringing in geese over land needs a bit more care, thought, and preparation than a water set because it takes more work to give the field set the realism of a water set. Most experienced gunners hunt with at least 100 decoys, although some use only a few dozen—but they must work harder to make the decoys appear more real. Much depends on the hunting pressure in the area and how far into the season it is. There are four types of decoys for field shooting: nesting, silhouette, folding, and full-bodied.

The lightweight, plastic-shell nesting decoys are by far the most popular with field goose shooters. The heads of these decoys are removable for carrying or storage, and the hollow bodies nest nearly inside each other. The heads and stakes are carried separately. These decoys are relatively inexpensive and lightweight, so a great number can be carried in to a blind.

Silhouette decoys are also very popular. These can be purchased or made at home, and are constructed of plastic, hardboard, plywood, or fiberboard. They are the least expensive, but also the least successful when used by themselves. The heads are usually movable to give different positions, such as feeding, sentinel, etc.

Folding decoys are very similar to profile decoys except that they unfold to give a more three-dimensional appearance.

Full-bodied decoys are the most expensive but also the most realistic and the most likely to bring in small flocks of birds. Some of these field feeders and sentinel decoys are made of molded plastic and even have feathering details. One great "confidence" model stands atop a stake on a plastic mound of mud. The goose is hinged to the "mud" stake, and even the slightest breeze causes it to move back and forth.

To make up such a large display, most hunters use a good number of silhouette decoys, but some full-bodied decoys should be mixed in with them. If you use silhouettes only, make sure that you have some of them turned at quarter angles from the main body so they won't become lost when the flight passes directly over them.

Geese always land and feed into the wind, so the majority of your decoys should also head into the wind. Mix up the decoys, using a lot of feeders, as well as loafers and sentinels or upright heads. The sentinels should be on the outside edge of the flock, preferably on the highest ground. The flock should be well spread out so it doesn't appear bunched up and ready for flight.

LAND AND WATER GOOSE DECOYS

Full-bodied decoy, hinged at the feet, on a plastic rock—
a great confidence decoy.

A hollow snow goose decoy.

A hollow shell Canada goose decoy,
with head in feeding position.

Some of the better field decoys can
also be used as water decoys by the
installation of a simple float.

Field goose set.

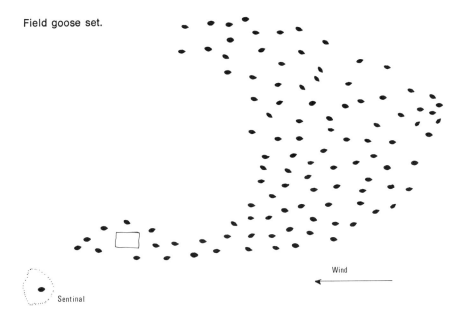

Wind

Sentinal

Hunting snow and blue geese requires even more decoys than hunting Canadas. Many hunters like to supplement their decoys with white cloths, such as baby diapers, or even newspapers placed on sticks pushed into the ground. These cloth tents seem to be effective and can often be used alone if it is early in the season and the geese haven't been shot at too much.

Decoys Over Water

Geese are highly gregarious birds, and the more decoys you have the better your chance of pulling them in. On the water the gunner should not use fewer than four dozen. If smaller groups of decoys are used, the geese may come in but they will circle and circle, usually just out of gun range. A few field geese placed in feeding or loafing positions on the shoreline will also help in giving a reassuring look to the decoys. The blocks should be placed with an opening in the center of the set and just in front of the blind.

Water decoys are full-bodied and may be hollow plastic shells or solid plastic forms.

Goose decoys naturally require heavier decoy lines and weights than duck decoys because of their greater size and weight. Large mushroom anchors are useful, as are big drinking cups poured full of concrete, with a ring buried in the top of the cup.

A typical goose set on a river sandbar seen from the blind.

RIGGING DECOYS

There is almost as much argument about rigging as there is about decoy pattern, and each gunner seems to have perfected his own system.

It is important to know the average water depth in which you are to place the decoys. There is no need for 50 feet of line in a 2-foot-deep mudflat. Always keep a little excess line on the keel. This can be wrapped around the keel and held in place with a large rubber band, or even half-hitched around the keel.

Carrying a good decoy set to and from a blind can be a terrible ordeal unless you have some sort of system. Sacks usually get thoroughly wet and freeze up, and boxes add extra weight that you definitely don't need.

Shown in the photos is a method developed by Bill Harper, a professional duck guide. This system leaves your hands free for carrying your gun or other items. The only items you'll need are large rubber bands cut from bicycle inner tubes. The rubber bands are used to hold the decoy anchor and cord in place.

CARE OF DECOYS

Decoys take a lot of punishment. Before each season they should be patched and repainted, and new keels, anchors, cords, and swivel rings attached.

BUILDING DECOYS

Making your own decoys can be half the fun of hunting. Not only is the thrill of decoying magnified a hundred times when you have carved the decoys yourself, but it's also a great way to spend the winter.

Making profile goose field decoys is relatively easy. You can use a coping saw, saber saw, or even a band saw. They are cut from thin wood (such as ¼-inch marine or exterior plywood or tempered hardboard), then painted with dull, flat decoy paints.

Carving your own full-bodied decoys—whether ducks or geese—takes a bit more doing but is actually quite simple. Use pressed cork for the bodies and chunks of white pine 2 x 4's for the heads. (The cork is available from Rector Mineral Trading Corp., P.O. Box 427, 9 West Prospect Avenue, Mount Vernon, N.Y. 10551. Decoy painting kits are available from Herter's Inc., Waseca, Minn. 65093.)

Granulated cork is available in 4 x 12 x 36-inch sheets. It comes six sheets to a package, and if you make the oversize 14-inch-long decoys shown here, one package will make two dozen decoys. Or you can make one dozen large full-bodied goose decoys from a package.

Enlarge the squared drawings and make full-size patterns, then cut the cork sheets into rough shape. Cut the ¼-inch hardboard bases to the lengths shown round their edges, and glue them to the cork. Use only a good-quality waterproof or marine glue. Shape the decoy bodies with a rasp or coarse sandpaper. Cut the heads, and carve to shape. Glue a ⅜-inch dowel in place. On the mallard bodies, drill a ⅜-inch hole in the top and glue the head in place, filling and sanding the joint smooth where the neck and body meet. On the goose decoys, drill the hole and push the doweled head in place; it can then quickly be removed for storage or transportation.

Sand the decoy bodies smooth and paint in the pattern of the species you have selected, using paints from a decoy paint kit. (These kits have especially formulated dull paints that are numbered to match a chart.)

Glue the keels in place and attach the eyes and anchors.

TWO EASY METHODS FOR CARRYING DECOYS

Decoys can be carried easily if they are fixed using this method: Pull the decoy anchor line out to about 12 inches or to the tail of the decoy and make a loop.

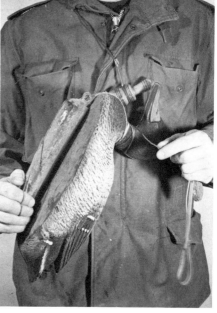

Take the line and make several wraps around the decoy head to take up the line.

Tie the rubber band onto the anchor line and pull it down over the tail of the decoy.

Pick up the decoys by the loop of anchor line and carry them by looping them over your arm or gun barrel.

Another way to carry decoys is in a nylon mesh bag which, unlike the sacks traditionally used for decoys, doesn't become heavy when wet.

PATTERNS FOR MALLARD AND GOOSE DECOYS

Profile of a cork goose decoy.

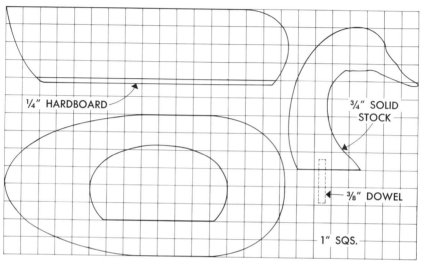

1/4" HARDBOARD

3/4" SOLID STOCK

3/8" DOWEL

1" SQS.

Profile of a cork mallard decoy.

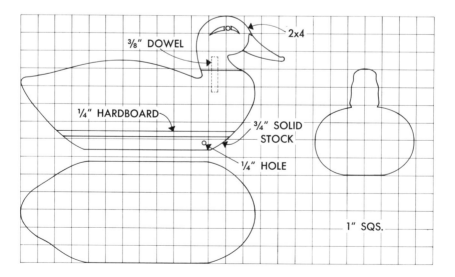

3/8" DOWEL

2x4

1/4" HARDBOARD

3/4" SOLID STOCK

1/4" HOLE

1" SQS.

ASSEMBLING A DECOY

The first step in making cork decoys is to cut the cork to shape, using a coping saw, hand saw, or band saw.

Cut a piece of tempered hardboard to fit the cork decoy bottom.

Glue the hardboard to the cork, using waterproof glue.

Shape the decoy.

Cut and carve the head to shape and glue it in place.

Use a good set of dull Latex decoy paints.

MALLARD

BLACK MALLARD

PINTAIL

BLUE-BILL

REDHEAD

CANVAS-BACK

GOLDEN-EYE

FRESH-WATER-COOT

SNOW GOOSE

CANADIAN GOOSE

1 Drake Mallard Bill.	14 Black Mallard Bill.	26 Pintail Drake Head.
2 Decoy Green.	15 Black Mallard Head.	27 Pintail Drake Gray.
3 Drake Mallard Breast.	16 Black Mallard Body.	28 Pintail Hen Body.
4 Drake Mallard Gray.	17 Bluebill Bill.	29 Pintail Hen Brown.
5 Wing Gray.	18 Spectrum Gray.	30 Redhead Bill.
6 Light Gray.	19 Barred Gray Back.	31 Redhead Head.
7 Wing Blue.	20 Hen Canvasback Brown.	32 Golden Eye Hen Head.
8 Decoy Black.	21 Hen Canvasback Sides.	33 Golden Eye Drake Head.
9 Decoy White.	22 Canvasback Bill.	34 Snow Goose Bill.
10 Hen Mallard Bill.	23 Drake Canvasback Head.	35 Canadian Honker Breast.
11 Hen Mallard Body.	24 Coot Body.	36 Canadian Honker Sides.
12 Hen Mallard Brown.	25 Pintail Bill.	37 Canadian Honker Back.

MAKING ANCHORS

Making anchors for your decoys is also relatively simple. They can be made by pouring concrete into large drinking cups and embedding an anchor cord ring made from a screw-eye before the concrete sets up. Or you can pour melted lead into a small ladle, placing a loop of aluminum clothesline in the lead before it cools. The loop should be large enough to fit over the decoy head. When the lead cools, it will shrink, and the anchor can be dropped out of the ladle.

One of the easiest anchors to use is merely a long thin strap of lead with a hole in the end. This can be wrapped around the decoy neck when picking up and storing the decoys. This system is used by many state waterfowl hunting areas that rent decoys.

You can also make your own plastic decoys using one of today's forming kits. The kits consist of aluminum molds and two plastic chemicals that are poured together, mixed thoroughly, then poured into the aluminum molds. Place the molds in your kitchen oven and the result is decoys of solid foam plastic. Easy and quick, all that remains is to paint the decoys using decoy paints.

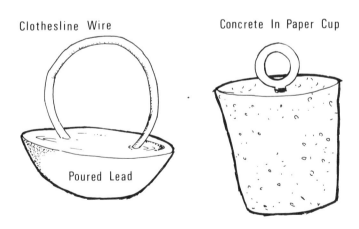

Two common anchors which are easy to make at home.

Opposite page:
A typical decoy painting chart of the type enclosed with painting kits. The chart indicates the many colors used on decoys and their proper placement for some common species.

MAKING PLASTIC DECOYS

Plastic decoys can be made, like this mallard, in your kitchen oven by using a kit. (Kits include metal molds, pour-in plastic, and decoy paints.)

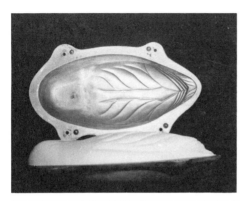

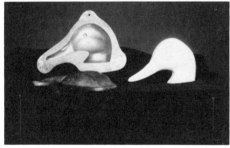

6

Blinds

Many old-timers believe that the single most important factor in success-ful duck or goose hunting is a good blind—one that blends in with the terrain and conceals the hunter properly. A good blind should also have room for easy shooting and be within calling distance of waterfowl fly-ways or "trading areas."

Blinds can be made from materials available at the blind location or assembled and transported to the location. A waterfowl blind can be anything from an elaborate concrete room to a pile of brush or reeds that the waterfowler can hunker down into. I once shot out of a blind in a private club in Kansas that not only had a telephone service back to the clubhouse but a pretty girl to deliver sandwiches when you called for them. About two weeks later, I was lying on my back in 2 inches of cold, wet Missouri cornfield mud with a camouflage cloth spread over me, waiting with a pounding heart as a flight of Canadas slowly settled into the decoys.

There are permanent, semipermanent, and portable blinds. Perma-nent blinds include field pits for goose or duck hunting, sunken water blinds, and shoreline, above-water blinds (also called stake blinds).

A good blind or other means of hiding is essential, whether the waterfowler hunts open water, potholes, river sloughs, or vast grain fields. This pothole blind near a cornfield is barely visible on the surrounding terrain.

Sometimes the best blind is no blind at all. This hunter achieves natural cover by kneeling in marsh hay.

Semipermanent and portable blinds are built for shoreline, shallow water, and boats. A good two-man blind is usually 3 x 6 feet and from 4½ to 5 feet high, with the seat 19 inches off the floor.

BLIND LOCATION

The location of a blind is its most important feature. If there aren't any ducks where your blind is located, naturally you won't get any shooting.

Get out in the marsh or water well before the season and scout out likely-looking areas for blind locations. Watch for early migrators or local ducks congregating in an area; usually the same areas will be used by the large flights of later migrators as well. In open water or large bodies of water, points of land that protrude out into the water are usually good choices for blind locations.

Don't confuse spring areas with fall areas. They are very often different, as I found out the hard way a few years back. Early one spring I happened on a huge flight of ducks using a small backwater slough. The next fall I arranged to lease the slough from the farmer who owned it, and hunted the area hard for several weeks without getting a single duck.

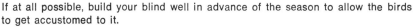

If at all possible, build your blind well in advance of the season to allow the birds to get accustomed to it.

I saw a lot of ducks, but they were using an area a quarter mile away, and I just couldn't call them in. When I mentioned this to the farmer he said that the area was always full of ducks in the spring, but he couldn't figure why there never were any on it in the fall. So the best bet is to do your scouting for blind locations just before the season opens.

Small islands on inland lakes are great spots for duck blinds, especially if they are set up where the lake narrows. Another good location on inland lakes is the flooded creek channels of their upper ends. The standing timber usually left in these old channels makes an extremely successful spot for a blind. Ducks normally use the rivers as travelways, often continuing to do so even if the rivers are interrupted by lakes.

Always locate a shoreline blind as close to the water as possible, since ducks don't like to fly over land if they are near water.

A stake blind or boat blind can be placed almost anywhere. Trading or travel areas between food locations and resting or rafting areas are excellent. The nice thing about a boat blind is that if the ducks start using an area some distance from you, you can always "pull up stakes" and move to where the ducks are.

Naturally, sunken water blinds must be placed in shallow water where there is no danger to the hunter from waves or flooding. Prime places for these blinds are in potholes or flooded timber country. They can also be used at the ends of small duck lakes, and work very well on flights of birds that have been shot at or spooked by other blinds on the lake.

A permanent blind should be constructed well in advance of the season so that the arriving ducks and geese become accustomed to it and accept it as part of the landscape. It's easy to over-shoot a permanent blind so it's best to have several, changing them frequently. If you do switch from blind to blind, give each one more resting than shooting days. Many hunters with permanent blinds like to hunt them in the morning only, letting the ducks use the area for rest in the afternoon. In this way you will have more shooting the full length of the season, even on small lakes.

BLIND CAMOUFLAGE

How you camouflage a blind is almost as important as its location. If at all possible, use materials gathered near the site so the blind will blend in with the surrounding vegetation, rocks, or soil. Do not take materials from the immediate area because they will make the camouflage blind

Materials for camouflaging the blind should be gathered from nearby to simulate the surrounding. These two young hunters are placing willow cuttings around a flooded river blind.

itself stand out, and the fresh-cut stubs show up like white flags. Which brings up another point: when I'm cutting brush to cover a blind, I like to stick the fresh-cut ends in the mud, covering the white ends. Then I place them on the blind.

For permanent blinds, many hunters like to plant climbing vines such as honeysuckle or even wild rose bushes for concealment. These living blinds can provide some great shooting without much additional camouflage, especially in the early parts of the season.

As the season progresses and hunters crawl in and out of the blind, the camouflage materials become weathered and worn. They should be spruced up or replaced to keep the blind properly concealed. Almost everyone knows that late season ducks are much more wary than earlier ones, yet most hunters give their blind camouflaging less attention at the middle or end if a season than they do at the beginning.

Willows cut and stuck in the mud are good natural camouflage materials, and they will last most of the hunting season if "planted" in this manner. Other good camouflage materials are marsh hay, slough grass, and the leafy boughs of cedar, oak, or other trees from the blind area. Rocks and even dirt can be used for camouflaging. In a muddy marsh I like to smear mud on the blind—when it dries, it blends in naturally with the surrounding area. It is also a good idea to keep a couple of old burlap sacks in your blind, which can be used for quick patching or for covering a boat motor or some other bright object.

The area around the blind should be policed regularly for spent shot shells or even dropped cigarette butts that may flare up and spook the ducks.

You'll need a hand scythe or ax for cutting camouflage materials and a shovel, also a roll of binder twine, wire, hammer, and nails for building and repair work.

A good way to attach camouflage materials to wooden blinds is to place screw-eyes every few feet at several levels around the blind. Binder

A good blind blends in so well it is hardly noticeable even as close as 50 yards.

twine can be threaded through these eyes, and marsh hay or even small branches pushed in and tied to the blind.

Metal or concrete blinds can be camouflaged easily if they are first covered with hog wire. You can attach almost any kind of camouflage material to this, using binder twine or wire.

If at all possible, the blind should be well camouflaged before the hunting season begins, so that there is time for it to weather, and for the ducks to grow accustomed to it.

TYPES OF BLIND

Permanent Stake (Above-water) Blinds

Stake or above-water blinds are usually located in open water, in the shallows of large lakes and bays, in the center of large marshes, or just off points of land on large lakes. They are supported above the water by pipe

Stake blinds are often used in public hunting areas, like this one in northern Missouri.

or timber pilings sunk into the lake or marsh. Most of these blinds are accessible only by boat, and they have space under them for boat storage.

Stake blinds are normally quite large and can usually accommodate four to six hunters. They take a lot of time and expense to build, but if located in the right area they can make for some mighty comfortable and profitable shooting year after year.

One bad thing about stake blinds is that in many states they are considered "open blinds." Although you may have constructed them yourself, they are available to everyone on a first-come-first-served basis if they're on public land.

Boat Blinds or Floating Blinds

Blinds constructed on many large inland lakes must be removed after each waterfowl season, so a good choice for hunting these areas is a boat blind. Boat or floating blinds are just that: large floating rafts with small camouflaged buildings to conceal the hunters. They have an opening in the center that you drive your boat into. Size varies a great deal. The old-time floating blinds had sleeping and eating quarters, storage space for boats, and a front and back shooting porch so that hunters could spend several days following the huge concentrations of waterfowl.

A boat blind is as effective as an above-water blind, even more so in many cases, since it can be moved and anchored in deep water close to rafting ducks. The floating part of the blind is very similar to the small

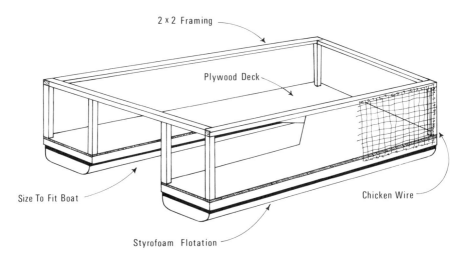

Floating blind.

Boat blinds such as this portable camouflage netting blind can often provide great shooting. Some boat blinds provide full camouflage for the boat as well.

private boat docks found all over inland lakes. It may be supported by empty barrels or drums or styrofoam chunks. Foam chunks make the best flotation.

Because of the great number of hunters in the marsh these days, waterfowl rarely stay in one place as long as they used to, so the luxurious "shooting palace" is no longer a successful cover and can really be considered a thing of the past. But the floating blind definitely is not outmoded; a small version, with just enough space to squeeze a boat into, or even shooting from a camouflaged boat, can work extremely well. When the ducks move to another area and the shooting drops off, just pull up anchor and follow the action.

Permanent Shoreline Blinds

Permanent shoreline blinds may be constructed in any number of styles and shapes and from all different kinds of materials. Wood, metal, or concrete are most commonly used, but blinds may be made from piles of rock cemented together on a rock point jutting into a bay—or even from a pile of logs lashed together on a high point in flooded timber.

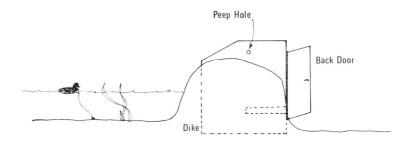

Peep Hole

Back Door

Dike

Permanent shoreline blind.

Some blinds may be sunk into the ground a little to give them a lower profile. If a blind is located on a dike or dam, the front opening is often slightly above ground level and the back may be completely open, with a door for easy entry. Blinds set in place on a dike or dam are usually made from poured concrete or metal and are large enough for three or four men.

Semipermanent Shoreline or River Blinds

Semipermanent shoreline blinds are very similar in shape to the permanent ones. They are generally constructed from wood, however, and may either be built first, then hauled to the site, or else built right there.

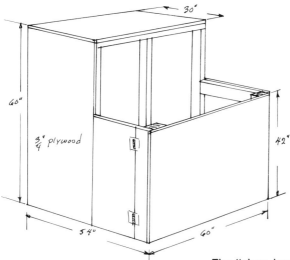

30"

60"

¾" plywood

42"

54"

60"

The "piano box" blind is the most popular semipermanent shoreline blind. This one is made of plywood and is mounted on a platform supported on pilings.

For years a good friend of mine who owns and operates a duck hunting club has constructed these blinds on runners like giant sleds. He can then haul them out and pull them back to his shop for repair, or move them around each year according to the food and water distribution. They are easily dragged on the dikes by using a small tractor. Many state fish and game departments are also using these "piano" blinds. They can be constructed from pre-cut marine plywood or slabs of rough-sawn green lumber nailed to a 2 x 4 frame. My favorite material is rough-sawn lumber. Plywood must be painted a dull color and will eventually separate, whereas the rough-sawn slabs will quickly fade to a dull gray, and though they will warp and twist, if they are a good hardwood like oak, they will last practically forever.

A couple of years ago I hunted with a group of young men who came up with an unusual, semiportable duck blind. The blind was light and easy to assemble, yet it was a sturdy weather breaker and provided excellent concealment. It was just perfect for hunting areas like public lakes where blinds must be taken down after each season.

The secret of the blind was in its construction and materials. It was made like a prefabricated house—we simply assembled the pieces on the site. For building materials we used discarded warehouse skids, which

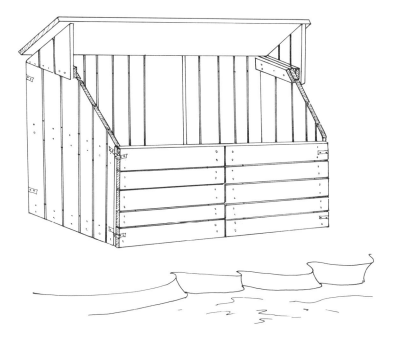

Paper-skid blind.

saved both time and money. Skids are usually free for the hauling. Paper companies, furniture companies, printing houses, and a lot of other people pay to have them taken away, so with a little asking around, you'll be able to make quite a haul.

Skids come in all sizes, but by experimenting we discovered that 38 x 50 inches makes the best blinds to seat three hunters comfortably.

For the blind you'll need:

2 skids for the sides
2 skids for the front
2 skids for the back
$1 \times 12 \times 8$ for the top
2×12 cut to fit for the seat

Lay two skids on edge lengthwise for the front of the blind, stand two skids on end for the sides, and two on end for the back. The two for the back, if placed at each end, will leave just enough space for a door. Cutting off the front corner of each side skid and nailing it in reverse to the back creates more headroom. Nail or wire a 1 x 12 to each side skid and to the two back skids to form a narrow roof. Nail cleats to the inside of the two side skids to hold a 2 x 12 board for a seat. If you wish, lay two skids down to make a floor; we prefer to fill our blind with marsh hay gathered on the spot. If you locate your blind in water, stake down the corners using 2 x 4's.

The skids are sorted, cut to size, and painted a good dull brown, and the seat cleats are nailed in place. Then everything is carted off to the blind site, and the skids are nailed or wired together to form the blind. We also use strap pipe hangers to help hold the blind together.

Flooded Field Blind

One extremely effective permanent blind is the field pothole blind. Because it requires a great deal of time and money to build and install properly, this should be placed on land you own or have a long-term

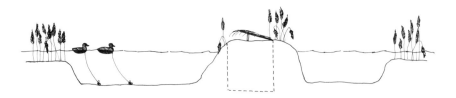

Flooded field blind.

lease on. In agricultural areas, especially those near waterfowl refuges, it can be one of the most comfortable and successful blinds for shooting both ducks and geese. Often these blinds are built and managed by grain farmers since they must be near a large grain supply.

The flooded field blind is basically a mound of earth in the center of a large flat field. The field is planted in some grain crop such as millet, rice, or milo that is attractive to ducks. Just before the season opens, the field is flooded by irrigation ponds or pumps from nearby rivers. The water level is kept just below the heads of the grain and provides excellent feeding for all kinds of waterfowl. The area around the blind mound is usually left unplanted for 35 yards, which leaves open water to place decoys and a good debris-free area for retrieving kills. An open version of this blind is the sunken pothole field blind. For this the area right around is dug somewhat deeper than the rest of the field. Usually only the pothole and nearby portions of the field are flooded. The blind itself is sometimes seeded in grains to conceal it.

Sunken Water Blind

One highly productive blind, although requiring a very specific location, is the sunken water blind. Some of the best duck hunting I have ever experienced has been from a concrete blind in a small clearing of 1,000 acres of flooded timberland.

This mighty comfortable blind is sunk about 1 foot into the mud,

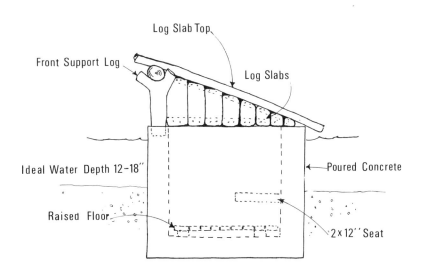

Flooded timber (sunken water) blind.

and each year when the timber floods the blind sits in about 18 inches of water. The top is covered with logs and log slabs and blends in superbly with the flooded timber. The river usually floods quite high, then drops, leaving the blind full of mud and water which must be bailed out and cleaned up before it can be used. But this problem is minor considering the comfort of the blind.

Sunken water blinds located in more open water are often called "tank" blinds because they are usually made from discarded metal tanks weighted in place. Tank blinds are extremely effective at the ends of lakes. It is a good idea to locate one at each end; then, depending on the wind direction and the flight patterns of ducks leaving and entering the lake, you can choose the better situated blind. One problem with these blinds is keeping them bailed out and dry enough to shoot from; another is the cost and effort needed to install them. Also, sunken water blinds have a relatively short life if made from metal, because of the rusting. Before sinking the metal tanks, you should coat them with black asphalt to help prevent rusting. Many blinds are built from concrete, but these require more expense and effort.

Goose Pits

The best blinds for hunting geese in the Midwestern grain states are pits dug into freshly harvested fields of milo, soybeans, corn, or other grain. They require a great deal of work, but can be extremely rewarding if well situated. The pits can simply be holes dug deep enough to conceal a hunter, or they may be more elaborate, consisting of metal tanks or wooden frames sunk into the dug pits. The tops of these blinds are usually movable and are covered with grain straw or corn. In some cases you can slide the tops back and forth to adjust them so that you can see out without the birds seeing you. On the more elaborate blinds the tops are hinged and flung back out of the way when the birds come in and you start shooting; such tops are usually made of lightweight wooden frames, covered with chicken wire and then camouflaged with grasses or corn stalks.

One of the problems with building and installing goose pits is that the dirt removed from the hole must be carried well away from the site so that the blind and field surrounding it remain flat and properly concealed. Wary waterfowl will quickly learn to detour around almost any discernible object in an otherwise flat grain field. In many cases after the season is over the blind must be removed and the pit filled, so that the field can again be planted in grain.

Field blinds for shooting geese are often elaborate sunken pits in which huge steel tanks are buried. Their tops are covered with sliding or hinged wooden hatches, which can be thrown back when shooting.

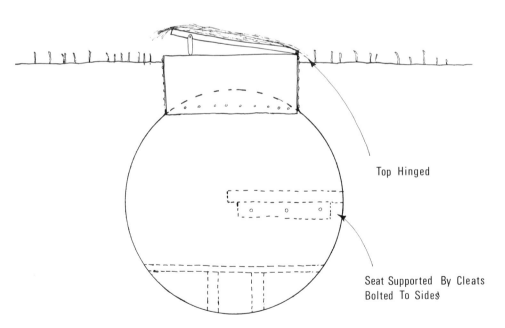

Top Hinged

Seat Supported By Cleats
Bolted To Sides

Tank goose pit.

Portable Blinds

A few years ago I had a good chance to see first hand how much fun a portable blind can be. I was hunting a public reserve in Kansas and saw several guys push a boat into a weedy flat a couple of hundred yards away. They pulled off a burlap bag that was covering a row of wooden slats and pushed these into the mud around the boat. For about 45 minutes they called to birds passing just slightly out of calling range, then literally pulled up stakes and went to the birds. Within half an hour I heard shots and watched as they both limited out in 45 minutes, packed up their blind, and headed home.

The value of these blinds is their maneuverability. They must be light enough to be carried easily to a good hunting spot, yet sturdy and heavy enough to provide the necessary camouflage.

I have two portable blinds, one large enough to place around my canoe or boat and one just large enough for one person to squat in. I keep the small blind inside my car all during the duck season; if I'm in a blind that doesn't produce, I'll fetch my portable blind and find a spot that ducks are traveling over so I can get some shooting.

A portable blind is extremely effective for hunting the public areas. You can make one of camouflage netting in a dead-grass pattern. The netting is stapled to wooden stakes, which are pushed into the ground around the hunter.

My blinds are made of 1 x 2 "tomato" stakes with their ends sharpened. I use six for the small blind and about a dozen for the larger blind, spacing them about 2 or 3 feet apart. To these stakes I staple a piece of field camouflage net in a dead-grass or field pattern. To give my blind a more natural appearance, I scoop handfuls of mud off the marsh bottom where I'm hunting and smear it into the material. The mud dries quickly and blends in quite naturally with the surrounding area.

Camouflage netting also makes a good portable blind. In a corn or wheat stubble field you can lie down and throw the camouflage net over you, again using the dead-grass pattern and adding a bit of mud to it. This can be very effective in places where geese and mallards are using the grain fields.

When snow covers the ground, an old sheet makes the best blind; if you are wearing one of the new white snowmobile suits, you can lie or squat in the snow and cover yourself with the sheet.

One excellent semiportable blind I hunted out of in Arkansas was made from lengths of burlap tacked around the crotch of a giant sycamore snag protruding from the middle of a shallow duck lake. We merely waded out to the sycamore and climbed up into the crotch; not the most comfortable blind but enormously worthwhile. The marsh had several blinds on both sides, and as the shooting became somewhat heavy all the birds started coming down the center of the lake directly at us.

Coffin Blinds

The unusual coffin blind was once a favorite with coastal shoreline gunners as well as with many gunners in the huge delta marshlands, though it has largely fallen out of favor today. Nevertheless, coffin blinds can be extremely effective in the right places. They are semipermanent in that they can easily be moved at the end of the season, even if they take some time to install properly and are hard to move during the season.

Coffin blinds usually accommodate only one man. They are simply shallow coffin-shaped wooden boxes that are sunk a few inches into the mud of a marsh dike or point of land. They are covered with a two-piece wooden hatch, which is usually grassed to match the surrounding area. These blinds should be installed well before the season gets under way so that the ducks become used to seeing them. Any dirt removed to place the blind should be carried a good distance away from the site. The inside of the blind is lined with clean, dry marsh hay; the hunter lies down in it and pulls the bottom hatch over him. As the ducks come in, he rises and shoots. When you are leaving the blind, remember to put the cover over it to keep out rainwater.

Coffin blind.

Sunken Barrel Blinds

The barrel blind is installed and used like the old-time coffin blind—it is simply a barrel or drum sunk into the sand or mud of a marsh or beach. These are so popular that they are now sold commercially.

Sunken barrel blind.

7

Boats

Boats and waterfowling go hand in hand, and the tradition of waterfowling boats is as old as the sport itself. Probably most every kind of boat has at one time or other been used for hunting ducks and geese. Some of the more traditional types include sculling boats, layout boats, double-ended punts, sneakboxes, and the first duck boats—canoes—used by the native Americans.

The main rule in selecting a duck boat is to choose one that is suited to your particular methods and the types of water you usually hunt. You wouldn't try to reach an open water floating blind in a canoe, nor would you plan to pole a huge runabout across a grassy flat. Waterfowling boats serve several purposes. They are used to transport gunners long distances through heavy seas to floating blinds or rocky islands, and to take hunters deep into swamps and sloughs. Some waterfowling boats also may be used as blinds, enabling the hunters to move swiftly to the best shooting spots.

Almost any kind of boat can be used for transportation, as long as it rises to the situation. Many hunters use their pleasure or fishing boats.

Boats have been traditionally used in waterfowling since shooting from a boat is an extremely effective method of hunting both ducks and geese.

On sheltered lakes and marshes where the primary job is to get to a blind back in a slough or pothole, the best choice might be a good johnboat. A johnboat is easy to row, takes a motor well, and is stable enough to be poled through shallows or narrow channels.

One of the best boats used in waterfowling is the "johnboat." This old-time Southern riverboat is ideal for slipping through flooded timber bottoms and marshy sloughs.

A push pole is used for moving duck boats through shallow, marshy areas. A duck-bill end opens against the mud and closes when drawn out, giving more leverage to the pole.

The size of the boat depends to a great extent on your hunting style. If you're a loner, you may need only a small boat to stow your gear and decoys. If you hunt with a dog, you'll need a larger boat. If you usually bring along a partner, the boat of course will have to be much larger. If two men, decoys, dogs, and gear are to be carried any distance, even on shallow, sheltered lakes, the boat should not be under 14 feet and it should have a wide beam.

Getting a boat through shallow water and narrow channels can be a real problem unless you pole it. A pole can be made much more effective by adding a duck-bill head, which is a hinged device that opens wide when pushed against the mud bottom, giving the pole more leverage. Pulling the pole closes the hinged jaws and allows the device to slip out of the mud easily.

With a little effort, some boats can be made into portable blinds. The boat shown here would be more effective if it was "grassed" or camouflaged.

Any boat used for waterfowling is more effective when camouflaged. To do this, paint it with a good, dull-colored flat paint—for example, a flat Latex exterior house paint. (Most paint stores carry several good duck boat paints.) To help break up the outline of the boat, you should apply the paint in irregular streaks and blobs in a random pattern. This camouflaging is much more effective if you use dull browns and tans, rather than the bright greens normally associated with camouflage colors; but the area you intend to hunt will dictate the colors you should use.

If your boat is wood, it's a good idea to give it a coat of fiberglass. In most Northern areas a great deal of waterfowling is done in icy water, which can really tear up a wooden boat. One layer of fiberglass cloth covered with resin can provide a lot of protection from sharp, jagged ice.

SCULLING BOATS

Also called sneak rigs or floats, sculling boats were once very popular with old-time Eastern gunners. They were used, as their name implies, for sneaking up on a raft of resting ducks. A single "sculling" oar protruded through the stern and was used to propel the camouflaged boat right into the rafting ducks. Most of these boats could accommodate two

Sculling boat.

men, and both the gunner and sculler lay in the bottom of the boat until they reached the rafting ducks. The gunners then raised up, one shooting to the left and ahead, the other to the right and behind. This was an extremely effective hunting boat during the days when hardy men made their living by shooting waterfowl that was sent direct to market, but it has largely fallen out of favor today. However, there are a few duck hunting camps with old-timers who know the art of silently sculling these slim, unobtrusive boats into an unsuspecting raft of bay ducks. Sculling boats are particularly effective on bluebird days, or those clear, bright sunshiny days when ducks raft up and just won't fly.

Sneak shooting rigs can also be used very effectively with a huge set of open water decoys. The gunners put out a large set of decoys a good distance from the shore, then return to the shore and wait, watching the decoys through binoculars. When a sufficient number of ducks have landed in the decoys, they start their sneak.

When used in open water, the sneakboat is normally tied to a buoy 100 or 200 yards upwind of the decoy set. Then when the ducks have landed in the decoys, the boat is cast off and drifted in, the stern sculler merely steering the boat.

On the Great Lakes, the sneakboats are somewhat different; there most of them have a hinged plywood shield or screen that hides the gunners. As the boat reaches the rafting ducks, the bow gunner throws down the screen and shoots.

In all cases the sculling boat or sneakboat is well camouflaged, often with pieces of driftwood or cedar boughs tied on to give the impression of a pile of floating debris. Some gunners place a carved seagull on the front of the boat to add to this impression.

LAYOUT BOATS

Layout boats are somewhat similar to the battery or sinkbox boats. (The latter, which actually placed the gunner below the surface of the water, have now been outlawed because of their excessive efficiency.) But in the layout boat the gunner lies just barely above the surface of the water, rather than below it as in the old-fashioned battery rig.

Hunting in layout boats is one of the most successful ways to bag open water ducks, but these boats are also illegal in some states, so check your local hunting rules. The gunner, in his tiny, flat, pumpkinseed-shaped boat, spreads a canvas spray apron all around him to prevent heavy seas from sloshing in. Usually a layout boat holds only one man because if it were large enough for two, it would defeat its purpose. Most layout boats are about 8 feet long, 4 feet wide, and 18 or less inches deep. A good layout boat, painted properly and with the decoys set in close to break up its outline, is almost impossible to see.

A second boat is normally used to transport the layout boat to the shooting location. One hunter stays in the layout boat and the second boat moves off—its job being to retrieve dead and crippled ducks. The hunters take turns in the shooting boat.

Generally, layout boats are not camouflaged. They are usually painted a dull color and depend entirely on their size and shape to blend in with the surrounding sea.

When the layout boat is used in open water, it requires a large rig of decoys—most gunners use at least 200—to cluster around and help break up its outline. The boat is usually anchored with the bow headed into the wind and the gunner lying with the wind. Depending on whether the gunner is left-handed or right-handed, the decoys are set with an open landing pocket to one side of the gunner. Although this rig is effective for hunting both divers and puddle ducks, the decoys should be kept separate in the rig, because even in a large raft of both kinds of ducks the two will be separate. Different species, such as bluebills, redheads, and "Cans," should also be kept separate.

A gunning day in one of these little boats can be enormously exciting. Since the boats are so tiny and the hunter lies so low in the water, he feels the next wave is surely going to take him. He may experience some discomfort, but the results should more than make up for all of it, because the shooting can be spectacular.

PUNTS

Double-ended punts have been popular with Eastern gunners for a long time, and their existence forms a large part of the tradition of Eastern market gunning. They come in all sizes, depending on the region, and often double as fishing boats. These traditional boats are extremely seaworthy; most of them are hand-made and passed down from generation to generation.

BARNEGAT BAY SNEAKBOX

Probably the most widespread of all waterfowling boats, the sneakbox is now sold commercially by several companies. The original sneakbox was designed and built in the early 1800s by a Captain Seaman of Barnegat Bay, New Jersey, a boat builder and avid waterfowler. Today's sneakboxes are styled on the old-time wooden planked boats, but they're made from molded fiberglass for greater strength and lighter weight.

Sneakboxes traditionally have round bottoms to conceal the boat and keep it low in the water. The curved upper deck covers the gunner and protects him from the elements. The cockpit has a hatch, which can be pulled up to give the gunner protection in bad weather or to keep equipment dry during transport. The deck curves down to the sides, allowing grasses and other camouflaging materials to hang into the water. A canvas spray shield can be erected on the front of the boat to protect the gunner even further from wind and waves.

There are several other advantages to the sneakbox: it can be powered by outboard, rowed, or even sailed; racks can be built on the sides of the deck to hold decoys; and the hatch can be fitted with a lock. In addition, you can stow all your gear, guns, and so forth inside during the trip to the shooting area.

The traditional sneakboxes were also rigged with ice runners. When the market gunners reached ice, they merely pulled the boat up onto it and set sail.

History has it that if heavy seas suddenly caught some of these old-time gunners unawares, they pulled up the hatch and let the little boat drift in to shore on its own. They often carried kerosene lanterns, and if they had to spend the night, they lit the lanterns and slept on the straw that lined the boat bottom.

One of the most famous waterfowling boat designs is the Barnegat Bay Sneakbox. Here is a newer version of the old-time sneakbox boat.

CANOES

Canoes have always been great hunting boats for slipping up on ducks and geese in small rivers, sloughs, and waterways. If your canoe is used only for fishing or hunting, you may wish to paint it in a camouflage pattern; but if you also use it for pleasure, there is another way of camouflaging it without ruining its appearance. You can buy a camouflage cover that will slip easily over your canoe—or you can make your own, using camouflage netting and a large drawstring around the bottom of the skirt. The gunners sit in openings in the skirt, much as you sit in a kayak cover.

American Indians used canoes for duck hunting, and they are still one of the best boats for hunting the small streams and lakes.

This is an effective camouflage for a canoe.

OTHER BOATS

Several other boats are used primarily for duck hunting, each of which is especially suited to its area. These include the pirogues or marsh boats of the Louisiana swamps, the traditional river johnboats used in the Mississippi River country, the Long Island Scooter boats, and the grass boats of the Northern lakes country.

Other boats are primarily duck hunting boats, like this marsh boat. Note the flat deck that can be used for grass camouflaging and for carrying loads of decoys to and from the blind. The long pole is used for pushing the boat through shallow water.

♂

♀

8

Guns

What makes the best waterfowling gun? Bring up this innocent question about two weeks before the opening of duck season and you'll get more answers than you can put into an encyclopedia. To most waterfowlers a gun is their trusty companion—one to share the good days and the bad. Many hunters feel that the only possible gun is a shiny new automatic; for others it may be a venerable, handed-down double with the barrel scratched and the walnut stock worn slick from use. According to the gun manufacturers, the most popular waterfowling gun is a twelve-gauge pump, full choke. But regardless of the kind you prefer, the best waterfowling gun is one with which you can consistently hit and kill waterfowl.

CHOOSING A WATERFOWLING GUN

There are basically three choices in waterfowling guns: automatics, pumps, and double-barreled guns. Each has advantages and disadvantages, and it's up to the individual gunner to decide upon the gun that works best for him.

Waterfowling guns are given the worst kind of punishment—being used in rain, sleet, freezing weather, and salt spray. Choose only the best, and maintain it properly.

Automatics

The automatic shotgun is chosen mostly because of its speed in getting off shots. You can shoot as fast as you're able to pull the trigger, without interrupting your swing or follow through. Most automatics come in a 28-inch barrel length, and the single sighting plane is easier for some hunters to work with. Automatics also carry three shells, giving that one extra shell that doubles don't have.

One of the major advantages of automatic shotguns is their minimal recoil. They come in one of two designs: the first, of which the Remington is an example, uses the gases from the spent shot to work the mechanism, and this definitely dampens the recoil. The second, a blowback style such as the Browning, uses the recoil itself to operate the mechanism—again cutting down on recoil tremendously. With less recoil to adjust to after each shot, naturally your string of three shots will be closer together in pattern. And when you're trying to bring down a big old goose, this can be mighty important.

The chief disadvantage of automatics is the problem of flying shells in a small duck blind. With some auto's, even new ones, you don't want to get on the right-hand side of the shooter or you'll end up ducking more spent shells than shooting at ducks. A second disadvantage is that it is hard to tell when an auto is loaded—a distinct problem in a crowded duck blind. The main worry, however, is that if the auto is not kept absolutely clean and almost free of oil during the freezing weather of a

Three of the most popular waterfowling guns: over-and-under, side-by-side double, and automatic.

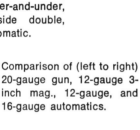

Comparison of (left to right) 20-gauge gun, 12-gauge 3-inch mag., 12-gauge, and 16-gauge automatics.

late waterfowling season, the gun oils may actually freeze it up and cause it to jam.

Pumps

The pump, or slide-action repeater, is the gun preferred by most waterfowlers. Very simple in operation, this gun is also very fast to swing and has a long, single sighting plane.

Many pump shooters can shoot almost as fast as a gunner with an automatic. The motion in operating the pump must become completely second nature to enable the shooter to keep a consistent string of shot and a smooth follow through. Pumps also carry three shells and are probably the most reliable guns in the field. They are lighter in weight than the automatics, but they do have a bit more recoil. Again, the chief disadvantage is in not knowing whether or not the gun is loaded without shucking out shells. Both the pump and the automatic shotgun are capable of holding more than three shells; but in the United States all guns must be plugged so they can carry no more than three.

Double Barrels

In the past the traditional double barrel accounted for more ducks than any other gun, but it fell out of style when the new automatics came into being. Today the doubles are making a comeback, and many older doubles are proudly being dug out of the closet and used again. Gun companies have once again started making them. Now you are quite likely to see a new doub e that greatly resembles the one in your grandfather's showcase, only the new one is guaranteed, with improvements in metals and mechanisms. The chief advantage of the double-barrel shotgun is the instant choice of two chokes. The double also has a desirable safety factor: you can quickly pop open the breech and know for sure whether or not a double is loaded.

One problem with doubles is that it is difficult to load them in the confines of a duck blind, particularly if you are using the over-and-under style. It must be "broke" deeply to insert the bottom shell, and this may require some masterful contortions in a crowded blind. Another disadvantage of the double is that it carries only two shots. With today's limits, though, you will probably pick a bird or two out of each flight, instead of shooting three or four as in the old days of big bag limits. So, for many waterfowlers, two shots is plenty.

The traditional side-by-side double has been the choice of waterfowlers for many years, but the newer over-and-unders are rapidly finding a place in the duck or goose blind. Over-and-unders are somewhat lower priced than side-by-sides, which can run into pretty high figures. To some hunters the wide sight plane of the double barrel is the easiest to use. This is particularly so if the gun is fitted with a raised rib and two sight beads which, once you get used to them, allow you to bring the gun into the same position quickly every time.

CHOOSING THE PROPER CHOKE

The choke is the restriction at the end of the shotgun barrel that causes the shot pattern either to travel in a tight bunched pattern—as in full choke—or to cover a wide area—as in open choke, used by many upland game hunters in extremely heavy cover.

In the old days a gun was often choked "full-and-full," and if you could drop a dime down the barrel of an old twelve gauge, you might just as well throw it away. Today most knowledgeable waterfowlers use a double-barrel gun with a full and modified choke, or even one modified and one improved cylinder. With the increasing emphasis on the sport of

SOME OF THE MORE POPULAR
WATERFOWLING GUNS

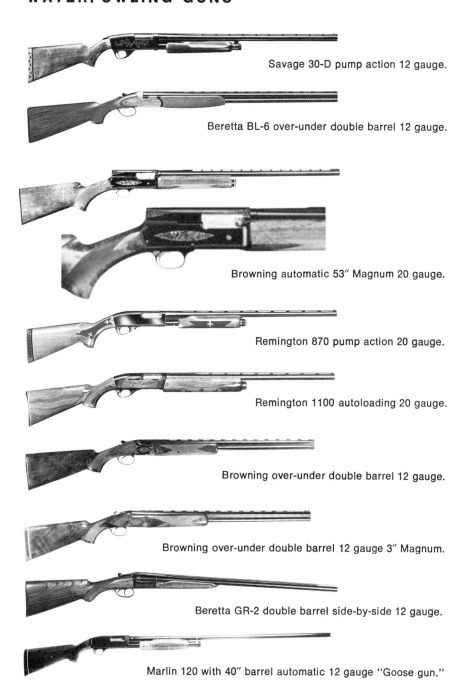

Savage 30-D pump action 12 gauge.

Beretta BL-6 over-under double barrel 12 gauge.

Browning automatic 53″ Magnum 20 gauge.

Remington 870 pump action 20 gauge.

Remington 1100 autoloading 20 gauge.

Browning over-under double barrel 12 gauge.

Browning over-under double barrel 12 gauge 3″ Magnum.

Beretta GR-2 double barrel side-by-side 12 gauge.

Marlin 120 with 40″ barrel automatic 12 gauge "Goose gun."

the hunt, waterfowlers do most of their shooting at distances which are much closer than those used in the old days. Shots at 35 and even 25 yards at decoying birds are actually the most common.

I shoot a double barrel side-by-side most of the time, with its choke full and modified. My first shot is the modified barrel at ducks coming in close and fast over decoys. The second barrel is used to bring down a cripple that I have winged, or as the birds have flared and turned away. Even when birds are within 25 yards after the first shot, they can flare and be 35 yards away in seconds as they quickly turn and head straight up in the air or zip to one side or the other.

Contrary to popular belief, the most effective choke for most of today's single-barrel waterfowl guns is a modified rather than a full choke. Some hunters like to put an attachment choke on the end of their barrel, such as the "Poly choke." Using this device, with a quick flick of the wrist they can change the choke to suit the occasion, whether they want improved cylinder for close-in mallards or pintails that are decoying beautifully within 20 or 30 yards, or full choke for shooting geese on those days when they just barely touch the killing range of 35 to 40 yards.

RANGE

Second only in importance to the proper choke is knowing how your particular gun patterns at different distances. Several years ago, I was hunting with a good friend who began calling a flight of sprig. I had just reached for a bottle of coffee in the bottom of the blind when he started talking to them. I held my position like a statue as he coaxed the wary, late season birds. "Let me know when to raise up and shoot," I said. After about 5 agonizing minutes, he yelled "Now!" and raised to shoot. I snapped out of my cramped position and also raised my gun. When I cleared the edge of the blind, a big beautiful bull sprig wasn't 25 feet from the end of my barrel. I pulled the trigger on the fast-swinging bird and missed him with both shots of my trusty old double barrel. Bill started collecting his ducks, and said, "Better throw away that old full-and-full double if you want to hunt with a good caller." He was right. At that range, my hard-hitting distance gun was carrying all its shot in about a 4-inch circle. A full choke gun will normally shoot 90 percent of its shot in a 40-inch circle at between 35 and 40 yards. The conscientious water-fowler shouldn't make shots at over 40 yards since the chance of crippling is much greater at this distance. It is easy to control your shots so they can all be at the 35–40-yard range by shooting over properly set decoys

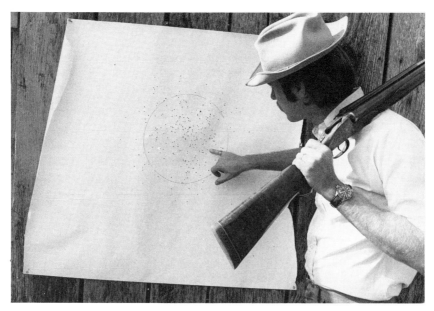

To be accurate with your gun, it is important to know how it patterns at different distances.

and making sure you have a gun that patterns best at the 35–40-yard distance. For most of today's modern guns and shot loads, this is a modified choke.

One of the most important points in waterfowling is to know the effective range of your gun at all distances. To do this, place silhouettes of ducks at about 30 feet and start shooting, stepping backward and shooting every 5 feet or so. Examine these patterns to determine at what distance your gun shoots best.

If you know your shooting range, you'll only go after what you can hit. The hunting amateur, weak in his knowledge of his gun, ends up sky-busting, not hunting. Sky-busting is a deplorable fact of waterfowling, especially in public goose hunting areas where there are numerous water-fowlers. Unfortunately, it is also contagious. Several years ago my wife and I were hunting a pit blind near Swan Lake. Our blind was situated on top of a hill high above the lake, and there were several blinds be-tween us and the lake. As the big Canadas began to lift off the water, the guns started bristling out of the blinds below us. It was a clear cold day, and most of the geese were flying from 60 to 100 yards high. Even so, they were followed up the hill by a barrage of lead. When they were directly over us, they were about 80 yards up. My blind was at least 100 yards away from the next, yet a couple of "hunters" below us were banging away at them. There were about ten flights like this. My wife and I never fired a shot, but she collected a crippled young goose that glided within 25 or 30 feet of our blind, after being shot at from a blind almost half a mile down the hill. The shooter never even attempted to retrieve his goose but continued to bang away as others flew over him. It was a terrible experience—one that we never want to go through again.

The fish and game departments of many states have tried to combat this problem by restricting the number of shells a hunter can take into his blind. In some areas the number is ten. The solution, however, still rests with the individual hunter. He should be able to judge distances, not only out away from him but also overhead. He should also know his effective shooting range and not take shots that are beyond it.

CHOOSING BORE SIZES

Traditionally, the bore most often chosen for waterfowling was the big twelve gauge; but with today's modern guns and magnum loads, the twenty gauges are just as effective at the 35–40-yard killing range as a maximum load of twelves. For many hunters, the lighter, easier-to-handle gun, and the lessening of recoil, are both innovations that have increased hunting success. After all, that's what it's all about; not how much punishment a man can take!

In the olden days of the market hunters, the cannons of nine and ten gauge were mighty popular. And still today you will occasionally hear the boom of a ten gauge on some goose hunting grounds, but I flinch when I hear it, even at a distance! Federal regulations limit the bore size today to no larger than ten gauge.

FITTING YOUR GUN

A shotgun is pointed rather than aimed; the hunter's eyes are actually the "rear sights" of the gun. For this reason a good consistent shooting gun must be properly fitted to the shooter. This means taking the gun to a qualified gunsmith and having him fit the stock to your shooting position and style. Many sportsmen do this but make the mistake of wearing light clothing. If you're going to be using the gun primarily for waterfowling, wear all your foul weather gear when you have the gun fitted. Then you'll have a gun that comes up more naturally and doesn't snag on your bulky clothes in the cramped quarters of a blind.

After all the discussion above about selecting your bore, choke, par-

PROPER SHOTGUN FIT

The main secret in good shotgunning is proper fit. This gunstock is too long, forcing the gunner to shoot too high. The butt of the stock is positioned too far out on the arm.

This stock is too short, and it places the gunner's face too near the breech for a proper sight picture. However, stocks for waterfowling should be shorter than those used for other hunting because of the additional padding of extra clothes.

A shooter with the right stock length has a perfect sight picture and brings up the gun naturally in the same position each time without undue effort.

An old-fashioned standard for testing stock length is to place the gun butt in the crook of the arm. The curve of the trigger should be where the last joint of the first finger hits. Other factors such as the length of the hunter's neck must also be considered.

To determine if the gun comes up properly, stand in front of a mirror, close your eyes, and bring the unloaded gun up into your normal shooting position. Open your eyes. You should be staring at a perfect sight picture.

ticular type of gun, and so on, it all comes back to the statement I made earlier in the chapter. Each hunter has to choose the gun that works best for him and that he can consistently and cleanly kill waterfowl with.

A hunt I made several years ago with a couple of friends brought this point home well. The three of us are about equal in marksmanship and all had spent many hours shooting waterfowl, often together. Yet each of us uses a completely different type of gun. I was shooting my favorite double, a twelve-gauge full and modified choked gun. The old double just seems to fit me right, although it is old enough that I can use only standard loads and no 3-inch magnums. The friend sitting nearest me was shooting a modified twelve-gauge automatic, using 3-inch magnums which he hand-loads, and with an extra amount of powder. My second friend was shooting his favorite, a twenty-gauge pump with a Poly choke attachment. He had pulled the choke down to full and was shooting 3-inch magnums.

At the crack of dawn, the first wave of geese started heading off their nightly resting waters and out to feed. The first flight was a little high and not too anxious to try our layout, so we waited. The second and third flights followed much the same pattern; but in about 15 minutes one flight dropped lower, made a slow circle, then started coming in toward our decoys. We gave a few anxious feed calls, then settled down absolutely quiet and still. Slowly but surely the big old honkers came on in. We were all experienced hunters, yet it was still tempting to rise and shoot, even though they were over 60 yards out, since they looked so big. But we resisted the temptation, and then on signal we all raised and fired.

The geese were about 25 yards straight in front of us, wings set for the slow descent, feet widespread to take the shock of landing. I fired first, and two shots sent the second goose on my side tumbling the remaining 25 feet to the ground. I heard the heavy thump-thump of the twelve gauge next to me and saw a high flier drop just at the edge of the decoys. The twenty gauge was still popping and the third shot dropped the third goose. We collected our three geese, a day's limit, and headed back to the car after a very satisfying hunt.

PRACTICE

One of the best things you can do to help improve your field shooting is practice. Shooting clay pigeons from a good hand trap or foot-operated trap is not only one of the finest ways to improve your shooting skill and find a fault that is causing you problems but a great Sunday

Waterfowling demands the best in marksmanship, and a few evenings spent trap-shooting can really improve your score in the field.

afternoon pastime as well. If you're using the trap to improve your field shooting, forget about traditional trap stances, positions, and so on. Try to position yourself just as you would be in the field, and vary the positions of the trap to duplicate the shots you would have at flying birds.

There are four typical shots that you'll never get a chance at with a conventional trap shoot. The first is a shot at birds that are coming directly toward you. To stage this shot, stand so that a small building (such as a garage) is between you and the trap thrower. Have the birds thrown high, directly over the building toward you. You won't see them until they clear the top of the building, and it takes split-second timing to connect. Needless to say, you should have the trap thrower well protected from falling shot, and should also make sure there is nothing else that can be damaged in the direction of the falling shot.

The second and third shots are much like skeet shooting, with a devious twist. I like to position myself hunkered down in a brushy fence row or a hedgerow. The trap thrower stands at one end of the row and throws directly in front of me, and occasionally overhead, varying the angle of the shots. Clay pigeons skimming the surface of the ground about 6 feet high and 20 feet in front of you highly resemble a fast-moving bluebill buzzing your blind, and even the best shots take a while getting on these birds. Again the trap thrower should be well protected from shot and concealed from the shooters so they don't know when the birds are coming. After you think you've got it down pat, let the trap thrower stand on the opposite side of the row, and you'll get to start all over again.

Often an old mallard will just pop over the top of your blind from directly in back of you and buzz the blind. To simulate this shot, you and a buddy start walking in front of the trap thrower and about 20 yards to either side of the clay pigeons. The idea is to bust the bird before your buddy does. Just keep walking and let the trap thrower toss the bird when he feels like it, which is usually when you're both as far off balance as possible. The bird quickly whizzes by and above you, making for one of the shots that are hardest to lead and yet often happen in waterfowling. A safety rule in this game is, of course, that you can only shoot after the bird passes you and is going straight away. A couple of guys shooting together on this can really have some fun.

Try as many kinds of field situations as you can dream up, and always have your gun down, safety on. In any shooting, safety comes first, so make sure there is nothing in the direction of the shooting, and always use commonsense caution. You'll soon be hitting birds you never thought you could connect with.

AMMUNITION

It takes at least a half dozen size 6 pellets to bring down a mallard, so you can see that proper range is very important. When shooting waterfowl, don't scrimp on the expense of shells. It takes a lot of shock and power to penetrate heavy feathers, down, and skin; using high-base shells will help improve your chances. Many shooters prefer to use magnums. These help by the increase in number of pellets they carry, although they don't (as many shooters think) hit harder.

Choosing Shells for Waterfowl

BIRD	FLIGHT SPEED	RECOMMENDED SHOT SIZE	CHOKE SELECTION	AVERAGE SHOT IN 30" CIRCLE AT 40 YARDS
Diving Ducks	48–75 mph	4, 5, or 6	Mod-Full	Mod 45–60% Full 65–80%
Puddle Ducks	35–65 mph	4, 5, or 6	Mod-Full	Mod 45–60% Full 65–80%
Geese	45–60 mph	BB, 2, or 4	Full-Full	65–80%

DUCKS
Use no. 4 shot for pass shooting. Use no. 5 or 6 shot for closer shots—for example, over decoys.

GEESE
Goose hunters need a lot of shock to knock down these birds, and so they use big loads and large shot. A gun that throws a dense pattern is extremely important. For average shooting, experienced hunters usually use no. 4 shot.

Again, the main idea is to fit the shot size to the situation. If you're shooting early season ducks, such as fast-moving small teal who haven't yet fully feathered out, you may even want to use 7½'s. This size throws a lethal pattern that is perfect for these small, fast-moving ducks, yet has enough killing power early in the season to warrant its use. As the season progresses, I switch to no. 6 shot for both ducks and geese. Both are decoying fairly close and it's easier to make head shots and good clean kills. Toward the end of the season, the waterfowl become more wary, staying farther away from decoys; they also feather out more, building up a layer of feathers to keep out the cold and wet that also keeps out shot to some degree. At this point I often switch to no. 5 shot for ducks and no. 2 shot for geese.

PICKING YOUR SHOTS

Regardless of how good a marksman you are, picking your shots is very important in waterfowling, just as it is in upland shooting. You can very often give yourself an edge just by shooting at the right moment.

For instance, decoying birds are easiest to hit just before they settle

When a duck has its feet out and wings set for landing, it is vulnerable because it has to change directions completely to make a getaway. Most gunners snap shoot in this situation, merely picking up the bird quickly in the gun sights, then shooting.

into the water. At this point they have almost stopped. They are much harder to hit when they take off from the water, because they shift gears and push off with some speed.

One good trick to help in judging distance is to set a particular decoy 35 yards away from your blind. You can then use this decoy as a reference point to determine the range of approaching ducks. If the ducks are outside the decoy, don't shoot.

If the ducks don't want to decoy but keep making inspection passes, wait until they just pass the outer edge of your decoys, straight in front, then try pass shooting them. If you shoot later, the birds will be swinging behind you, making for more difficult shots.

A successful waterfowler must discipline himself to pick out one bird from an approaching flight and keep shooting until that bird falls, before he starts for another. The experienced gunner becomes oblivious to all birds other than his target. Don't pick out the easy (normally the first) bird; choose the second or third, and work toward the front of the flight. "Doubling," or having two shooters connect on the same bird, is often caused by both shooters picking the easiest bird. You should also shoot only at birds on your side of the flight.

Watch cripples closely and retrieve them as soon as possible. Many a waterfowler has been frustrated to see a good, clean hit fall dead to the water, only to find that while he was taking a shot at a second bird, the "cripple" swam into the reeds, or even dived under the water and gripped a reed to stay down. Always take a loaded gun when retrieving cripples because you may have to make another killing shot. If it is necessary to make a second shot, aim for the head. A duck floating on water has most of its killing area submerged and can be extremely hard to kill. I always carry a few no. 8's for finishing off cripples, and the extra dense pattern really helps.

The speed of many geese and ducks is often underestimated. Remember to take this into account when you're getting ready to shoot. One particularly effective trick if you're going for geese on a quartering or swing-away shot is to aim at the lead goose. Surprisingly often your shot will crumple the second goose instead of the one you shot at.

WATERFOWL WING SHOOTING

There are three basic shooting systems used by most hunters: snap shooting, swing-through, and lead shooting. Most hunters stick with one system, although a good wing shot knows how to use all of them because each is particularly effective on specific types of shots.

Snap Shooting

Snap shooting—the method least used on waterfowl—is actually split-second reflex shooting. The shooter picks out a spot where he thinks the bird will fly, brings his gun into position, and shoots at the spot. This method is more often used in upland shooting at extremely fast-moving game, such as quail on a covey rise. It is also very effective when ducks are hovering over the water just before they sit down.

Swing Through

The swing-through and lead systems are more frequently used on waterfowl because it's easier to pick up and track the target with the gun barrel. In the swing-through method you pick up the target with the gun barrel, swing past it, then shoot. The amount of swing through is determined by the distance or lead you give the bird. The swing-through method is the best one for shooting at ducks over decoys.

Lead Shooting

The lead system involves picking a spot ahead of the bird, keeping the gun swinging ahead of it, and pulling off the shot. This method is often used in pass shooting because it is easier to get more lead for faster-moving ducks and geese.

GUN CARE

Because of the conditions inherent in their use, waterfowling guns receive some very harsh treatment. They are exposed to sleet, rain, freezing weather, and salt water. However, a good waterfowling gun can be a lifetime companion, giving consistent results, if it has the proper care.

Whether the gun is brand new or well aged, you must give it a good pre-season oiling and checkup, and take care of it well throughout the season. I like to wipe the outside metal portions with a good rust-penetrating oil, such as the one gun dealers use to protect their models during all the handling they get while on the rack. I dust-spray the inside working mechanism with WD-40, one of the best penetrating rust preventives. In my car I keep a rag well soaked with gun oil in a plastic bag; when I get back after a day's hunt, I carefully wipe down the metal, removing any rainwater or moisture. I don't like to case my waterfowling guns because of the moisture they pick up, so I wrap them in old towels for the trip home. They're then left in a gun rack so they have every opportunity to dry out thoroughly.

THREE BASIC SHOOTING SYSTEMS

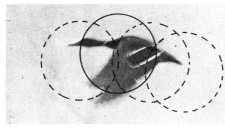

Swing through is the most consistent form of shooting: it involves picking up the bird with the gun barrel, swinging to the bird, shooting just as you pass it, and continuing in a smooth, even follow-through.

In snap shooting, the hunter, in a split second, approximates the spot where he expects the bird to fly and shoots at that spot.

Lead shooting is most often done in pass shooting for fast-moving geese and ducks because it's easier to pick up the amount of lead needed. The gunner here has picked the front goose and is leading it. If he misses, he might hit the second; if he shoots low, he'll get the lower goose. Picking your shots can mean the difference between filling a bag and going home empty-handed.

Before heading out for a day's hunt, spray the inside and outside of your gun with WD-40. Then wipe down the outside.

When you get back to your car from a day's hunt, wipe down the outside of your gun with a rag soaked in a good gun oil, such as Brownell's rust preventive.

One particularly bad problem with pump and automatic guns is sticking and jamming during freezing weather. It can be extremely frustrating to draw a choice blind and then have to watch flight after flight of geese come in while you curse a jammed gun. The problem in most cases is the wrong oil. If you plan to use your gun in freezing weather, it should be disassembled and all the old gun oil wiped carefully off. Then dust-spray each part with a penetrating oil, wipe off the surplus, and reassemble.

CAMOUFLAGE

Many hunters forget to camouflage their guns. They go to a great deal of trouble building and camouflaging a blind, and are just as particular about choosing the proper clothing to blend in with the blind and not spook the ducks. But the same hunters may be shooting a polished new gun that shines like a silver dollar. Devout shooters camouflage their guns. Camouflage tape like that used by archers for taping up a brightly colored bow is excellent; this material doesn't damage the gun in any way yet effectively conceals a long shiny barrel poking out of a blind.

Ernie Simmons—founder of the Simmons Gun Specialty Company in Kansas City and inventor of the ventilated rib—was one of the most dedicated duck hunters I ever met, and his duck gun was a no-nonsense pump sprayed with camouflage paint. When Ernie came up out of a blind, all a doomed mallard saw was a patch of brown and green—no shiny black muzzle.

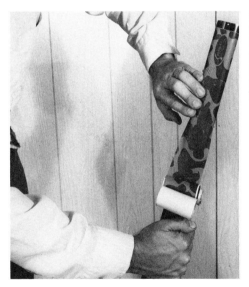

Camouflaging your gun can quickly be done with tape like the kind that archers use. This is easily removed at the end of the season and doesn't harm the gun in any way.

♂

♀

9

Dogs

Hunting with a good retrieving water dog is half the fun of waterfowling. What waterfowler doesn't thrill with excitement when his enthusiastic Labrador retriever jumps into freezing cold water and swims through chunks of sheet ice to pick up a crippled mallard that is slowly swimming out of sight, or glow with pride as a triumphant Chesapeake comes into the blind with his fourth successive retrieve?

A good water dog is not only a companionable and helpful aide-de-camp; he is also invaluable to wildfowl conservation. According to studies made by fish and game departments, almost one-fourth of the shootable waterfowl that comes through the United States dies from crippling and is lost or not picked up by the shooters. Practically every duck or goose hunter has experienced the frustration of making a good hit and watching the bird fall, then searching for an hour in heavy slough grass or reeds coming up with nothing, and then deciding to shoot another duck to replace the lost one. A good water dog can locate most slain ducks, thereby reducing the total number of birds actually shot and thus aiding in duck conservation.

Water dogs are individuals, and some of their antics and feats can

A good retrieving dog is worth his weight in gold to the sportsman who wants to insure bagging most of the birds he shoots and also wants to help waterfowl conservation.

provide moments you will cherish for life. I remember a jump shooting stalk a friend and I once made on a flight of about 1,000 mallards. It was early in the season, and we had spotted a huge flight working a tiny pothole in the center of an unharvested cornfield. Because the corn was so high we were able to make a crawling sneak right up to the ducks. The scene was so fantastic that we just sat and watched for half an hour. When my friend's Labrador saw all those ducks working in the water and trading back and forth in the sky above, she went absolutely out of her mind. She began to shake from waiting so long, her eyes started to roll, and she was chomping and frothing at the mouth. When we finally started shooting and ducks started falling, the Lab went to work under full power.

Another time Bill Harper and I were in a blind on a public lake, and he made a shot at a single, low-flying duck. He turned the duck sideways, and the old drake started slipping even lower and headed toward another blind a couple hundred yards away. We saw the bird fall, then heard the shot from the other blind. So did our black Labrador, who shot out of our blind like a cannon. She beat the dog in the other blind and proudly brought the dead mallard back to us. That required a 200-yard walk and a little apologizing.

Labrador Retriever

Popular with a great many waterfowlers, this beautiful dog originated in the Canadian province of Labrador and is a hardy, easily trained breed.

The Lab, as the dog is affectionately called by waterfowlers, is solidly built, normally standing from 21½ to 24½ inches tall and weighing from 60 to 75 pounds. The coat is very thick, straight, smooth and solid in color, usually black. Yellow is the second most popular color, but the breed exists in other solid colors as well.

Compared to most other retrievers, the Lab is broader in the hindquarters and usually somewhat shorter and more solidly built. The head is wide, smooth and clean, with no fleshiness. The brow is noticeable, and mouth and jaws long and powerful. The ears are not usually very long and are set close to the head, low and well back on the skull; the eyes are yellow, brown, or black. Neck and chest are powerful and well developed, and the legs extend straight from shoulder to the ground. The tail is round and smooth-haired.

The Lab is one of the most intelligent retrievers, easily trained to sit or lie still in a boat or blind. They are well-mannered and friendly, and make delightful pets. (They also make excellent Seeing-Eye dogs.)

The Black Labrador Retriever is the most popular of the retrieving breeds. He is intelligent, easy to get along with, and hard working.

The Lab is happiest retrieving downed game, whether from an icy river channel or a muddy cornfield. He can be used with other dogs without starting fights and will get along well with everyone in the blind.

Since a Labrador learns easily to hunt upland game in the flushing manner, it is a good choice of breed if you enjoy hunting both upland game and waterfowl, but are unable to keep a dog for each.

Chesapeake Bay Retriever

A favorite with the most hardy of waterfowlers, this rugged and aggressive breed comes from Newfoundland. Covered with a heavy, oily coat that enables the dog to work and enjoy even the coldest, iciest water, the Chessie is strictly a working hunter. They are larger and blockier than the other retrievers, for Chesapeake breeders have done what most other breeders have not: they have resisted any attempts to beautify the breed,

The hardest working of all retriever breeds, the Chesapeake Retriever is a great all-work-and-no-play dog.

so that it is strictly a hunter's hunter. The powerful body enables the Chesapeake to swim for a long time without tiring, and its fondness for water can be appreciated only by seeing this aggressive dog hitting the water. The Chessie is all work and no play; when it starts for a retrieve it goes with all the strength it has. Chessies are extremely intelligent and can mark several birds at one time, retrieving each one even under the most adverse conditions.

The Chessie has a very dense coat, colored anywhere from dead-grass gold to dark brown, so that it blends into a blind quite easily. The oily coat sheds water extremely well—when the dog climbs back into the blind and shakes off, everyone gets wet!

The Chesapeake is a real individual, somewhat harder to train than other retrievers. The breed's aggressive temperament usually makes it a poor choice for a house pet but a very good choice for a hunting dog. The Chesapeake normally doesn't get along with unfamiliar dogs or people. Some Chessies are quite hard-mouthed, although they can usually be trained out of this with a little effort.

Irish Water Spaniel

This unusual dog was originally bred to work the cold bogs and marshes of Ireland. The breed's thick, tightly curled coat protects it from even the bitterest cold. Unfortunately this coat is also the bane of the Irish, seeming to pick up every stick and burr it passes, and soon becoming a complete tangle of debris that is almost impossible to separate and comb out.

The Water Spaniel is either dark brown or black. Its most distinguishing feature is a ratlike tail—the breed is sometimes called the "rat-

The Irish Water Spaniel was originally bred to retrieve in the cold boggy marshes of Ireland.

tail" because of it. This tail is covered with short smooth hair, in contrast to the rest of the shaggy, curly coat.

The Irish is more sturdily built and larger than the other spaniels, weighing up to 65 pounds and standing from 21 to 24 inches high at the shoulder. The face is smooth and well featured, with long sloping jaws and a wide head with a noticeable bulge on top. The eyes are usually hazel to dark brown, large, set well apart.

The Irish is an extremely strong swimmer and loves the water. It is considered a one-man dog, being fiercely loyal to the master and often suspicious of strangers. This dog will not stand for hard training and should be coaxed rather than forced. The Irish may be a little hardheaded, but he/she really performs once he learns his lessons.

Curly-Coated Retriever

This is a great water dog, although it hasn't found too much favor in the United States. The Curly Coat is a beautiful animal, with tightly curled dark brown or black ringlets. Rangy dogs, they stand from 23 to 24 inches at the shoulder. They are usually somewhat lighter in body build than other retrievers, although quite sturdy and strong.

The head is smooth, wide, and well shaped, with long powerful jaws. The eyes are dark brown or black, wide and large. The ears are small, set well back on the head, and covered with dense curls. The tail is carried straight back and is fairly short.

The Curly Coat truly loves water and will swim for great lengths of time even in cold weather and icy water. He will dive for crippled ducks, a feat that makes him a top water dog in any hunter's book.

The breed is very intelligent and easy to train. These dogs have a

A beautiful dog with tight curly brown hair, the Curly-Coated Retriever hasn't found too much favor yet in the United States.

good memory and are even-tempered and companionable. Like most retrievers, they can also be taught to hunt upland game, although the curly coat can cause a great deal of trouble.

Golden Retriever

Considered by many to be the most beautiful and stylish of retrievers, the Golden ranks second in the United States among retrieving breeds. They do make great water dogs, but their fine silky hair will quickly absorb water, so that they don't have the ruggedness and ability to withstand extremely cold water and ice.

Goldens have a beautiful, richly colored, silky coat of long hair, usually light gold, although sometimes more like caramel or even dark red. The head is broad, with a wide strong jaw; the eyes are large, set well apart, and usually rimmed with dark brown; the overall facial expression is friendly. The body is well proportioned, long, and deep-chested, with a straight tail. The coat is fairly thick and may be either wavy or flat.

This breed is considered the best for nonslip retrieving or walking at heel until commanded to retrieve. Goldens are not usually as aggressive or stylish in the upland field as Labradors, although they normally make a somewhat better retriever. The biggest problem with the Golden is the coat, which absorbs water, catches burrs and debris, and requires much attention.

They more than make up for this, however, by their eagerness, and they are a superb choice for the one-dog sportsman who likes to hunt upland as well as waterfowl. Goldens are particularly capable in fairly warm climates, which are better suited to their physical abilities. They are good-natured and friendly, and make good pets. Somewhat softer-mannered than most dogs, they must be trained gently, with considerable understanding.

The Golden Retriever is a favorite of almost everyone, and his beautiful looks and stylish retrieves make him an excellent dog.

Flat-Coated Retriever

Once called the Wavy-coated Retriever, this excellent water dog has never been very popular in the United States. Very good-looking, fine-haired, with a well-shaped wide head, the Flat-coated Retriever is usually black or dark brown with dark brown or hazel eyes. This well-built, muscular breed's coat can withstand most any water and weather condition. It is a fine working retriever, a competent swimmer, and a great lover of the water.

OTHER BREEDS

There are several breeds of gun dogs that make excellent upland hunters and can also, with some training, be used for waterfowling. These dogs don't usually have the build, physical stamina, and heavy, dense coat needed for the hard work and icy conditions of waterfowling, but they can be worked in mild climates and occasionally even in cold climates.

Weimaraner

Although not very popular as a water dog, this breed works well on short retrieves in mild weather conditions and is often used by the one-

An all-around dog sometimes used for waterfowl retrieving is the Weimaraner. His short coat will not keep him warm in extreme weather conditions, but the dog is a good worker in milder climates.

dog owner who hunts both upland and waterfowl. The Weimaraner is an overall even gray in color, which is why it is often called the gray ghost. The coat is short, smooth, and dense, and the dog has a well-muscled appearance.

Wirehaired Pointing Griffon

For the hunter who likes both upland game and waterfowl, the Wirehair is a wise choice. The heavy coat gives these dogs good protection in cold water, and they are both accomplished swimmers and good retrievers. Quite small in build, the Wirehair is covered with short, bristly gray or brown hair.

German Wirehaired Pointer

This breed is distinguished by a coarse coat and whiskered face. Although basically pointing dogs, they can easily be trained for waterfowl retrieving, and the dense coat enables them to withstand the rigors of the job.

A good choice for the hunter who likes hunting both upland birds and waterfowl would be the Wirehaired Pointing Griffon.

Although the German Wirehaired Pointer is just that, a pointer, he can be trained as an excellent water dog, and his coarse, dense coat helps him combat the cold.

Springer Spaniel

The Springer Spaniel is primarily a flushing dog (one that quarters ahead of his master and flushes game), but with a little training he can become an excellent waterfowl retriever. These are quiet, gentle, friendly dogs that can make delightful home companions.

American Water Spaniel

Primarily a flushing hunter, the Water Spaniel can easily be trained to retrieve game, including waterfowl. A pretty fair multipurpose breed, they can be great family dogs.

The Springer Spaniel is often used by waterfowlers who also like to hunt upland game, and in mild climates this sporty little dog can provide plenty of action.

Another great multipurpose dog is the American Water Spaniel. He can be trained to retrieve waterfowl as well as upland game birds, and he also makes a great pet.

The Tolling Dog

Although not a recognized breed, the tolling dog is quite an unusual waterfowling animal. It is bred to resemble a small fox and its talent is in "tolling," or enticing, waterfowl into the gun. The small dog will parade up and down a stretch of beach or point of land and cause curious ducks to swim in closer. This odd way of hunting—and this unusual breed—are both favorites in Nova Scotia and other far northern areas.

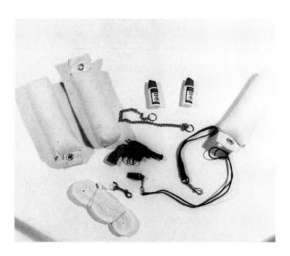

Some of the equipment needed to properly train a water dog—choke collar, gun, leash, whistle, training dummy, and duck scent.

TRAINING

To make a good companion and effective helpmate of your water dog, you must train him (or her) properly. There are two ways of doing this. You can send the dog to a professional trainer; or, if you have the time and patience, you can train him yourself. But you should not attempt this unless you are absolutely willing to go all the way, and plan to spend a lot of time with the animal. It's not fair either to the dog or yourself if you only try to train him halfheartedly.

If you decide to send your dog off to a trainer, you should in any case plan to spend a great deal of time there yourself as well. You have to learn how to recognize your dog's traits and faults, and to know exactly how he has learned to react to certain situations and to each command.

Home Training

If you have the time, training your dog at home can be a great deal of fun, and can make the two of you into ideal hunting companions.

Obedience is the key to training any dog well, and it is especially important with a water dog. This dog must be trained to lie still in a blind or the bottom of a boat while all kinds of exciting things are driving him practically crazy. One of the most annoying habits of a poorly trained water dog is breaking at the sight of ducks, which means you lose chances at ducks and probably ruin a few friendships as well. A good, well-rounded water dog will not only make the retrieves that he marks, but will also obey your hand signals as you direct him to birds he cannot see because of brush or high waves. A good retriever can also be trained to follow you as you make a stalk for jump shooting ducks.

You should get your puppy as soon as he's weaned and on solid foods, which can be anywhere from six to eight weeks from birth. Start familiarizing him with facets of hunting straightaway: take him for short rides in the car; play with him, throwing small sticks and dummies or a duck wing to bring back to you; and let him get used to retrieving in a quiet, shallow pond.

Whenever the puppy does anything you like, give him lots of affection and praise to let him know he has pleased you. Don't feed him dog cookies or other foods as a reward or you'll be doing this the rest of his life. The most important thing with puppies is to make everything fun. The puppy will do the rest.

Most trainers say that you can start training your dog formally when he or she is six to nine months old. That's where you have an advantage over the professional trainer. You have already been playing with the puppy and can introduce short lessons whenever he appears interested. But don't overdo it. Give the pup very small doses at first to match his attention span and to avoid wearing him out. By the time the dog is nine or ten months old, you should be working with him on practically every facet of obedience and hunting—and he should be responding enthusiastically to your training.

There are several rules for training dogs that can help you produce a well-trained, well-mannered, vigorous dog.

The first is to temper your training to your dog. Each arrival is an individual; before you can train him (or her) properly, you must get to know him well.

Make him obey your command without repeating it. This prevents the shouting matches that hunters get into with poorly trained animals. Once you give a command, be sure you follow through with it and make the dog do it. Use discipline—which is not the same as punishment—and enforce each command. Whenever you issue a command, try to make it in the same tone, and always give the same command for the thing you want done.

Never yell at your dog to get him to obey. He should be able to follow a command even if it is given in a low voice. You'll see how important this is when a flight of mallards is just starting into your decoy set.

Make sure the dog knows that you are unquestionably the boss—this rule takes a bit of work but is well worth it in the long run. You want a dog that can think for himself yet won't be ruling you.

Obedience Training

The first step in formal training is to put your dog through a sort of obedience school. He should be trained to the commands sit, stay, down, come, heel and kennel up. No punishment should be given if the dog doesn't do the job. Use discipline, but make sure he carries out the command properly.

SIT

Say the word SIT, and gently but firmly push down the dog's hind quarters. When he sits, give him lots of praise. Keep practicing this until the dog does it without the hand pressure. Use no punishment if he doesn't—just keep repeating the exercise.

STAY

The next logical step is to get your dog to stay after he has been commanded to do so. Place a choke collar on him and tie it to the spot where you have commanded him to stay. Then walk away. Do this until the dog will stay without following and without being tied to the spot.

After the dog has learned to stay, command him to SIT and STAY, then start throwing dummies out, again making him STAY at your side. The next step is to repeat the performance while standing some distance from the dog and having someone else throw the birds or dummies.

DOWN

This command is similar to SIT but tells the dog to lie down. It is very important for a water dog, since you may want him to lie down to break up his outline when a fast flight of pintails catches him out in the open away from the blind or other cover. Give the command DOWN and pull the dog's feet out in front, forcing him down. Repeat until the dog will go down without pressure.

COME

Your dog will naturally want to come to you when called, but he may also decide once in a while to ignore you. This is a fault that happens occasionally even with older dogs. A well-trained gun dog should come to you without hesitation. Place a choke collar and long leash on him, give the command STAY, and walk away, then command him to COME, gently pulling on the choke collar as you do so. If the dog balks, pull harder until he comes. The difficulty with this command is in getting a young dog to stick to it after being trained. If a young dog won't come, the owner will often start to move toward him. The dog immediately assumes he wants to play and will run away so that the owner will chase him. The answer is to turn and run away from him; he will quickly follow you. Then replace the choke collar and give the dog a refresher course.

HEEL

This command is very important for any dog, and usually quite easy to accomplish. Issue the command and hold the dog at your side with his head up. Walk and lead the dog with pressure from your hand. If he insists on walking in front of you, swing the ends of the leash in front of you. Having the leash snap his nose a few times will help remedy this problem. You must train your dog not only to walk by your side but also to watch you and turn as you turn, so that you don't bump into him.

A right-handed shooter should train his dog to heel on his left side; a left-handed shooter on his right side.

When your dog begins to pick up the obedience commands pretty well, you can start training him to retrieve properly and to follow hand signals.

KENNEL UP

KENNEL UP is to me one of the most important commands you can teach a gun dog. I hate to have to coax, pull, even lift a stubborn dog into an automobile, boat, or blind. KENNEL UP is the command given to instruct a dog to enter anything. The easiest method of teaching this command is to apply it first to something you yourself can get into, such as a station wagon back or the dog's kennel. If you are using a station wagon, get in the back yourself, with the dog on the ground attached to a leash. Give the command KENNEL UP, slap the floor of the wagon with your hand, and give a sharp tug on the leash. When the dog has learned to enter with you inside, stand outside beside him, slap the floor of the wagon, and give the command. Once the dog has mastered one place, you can go on

DOG COMMANDS

Sit—Give the dog the command *Sit* and gently push his rear end down with one hand while pulling his chin up with the other.

Stay—Give the dog the command *Stay* and step away. If he follows, take him back to the spot, make him sit, and repeat.

Down—Give the dog the command *Down* while he is sitting, then pull his front feet out in front of him, forcing him to lie down. Repeat this until the dog understands.

Come—Tie a choke collar on the dog and command him to *Come,* gently tugging him to you as you give the command. When the dog comes to you readily, remove the collar and repeat the command. If he doesn't come, turn and walk away.

Heel—This command is taught by placing a choke collar on the dog and leading him by your side. Give the command *Heel* and pat your side. Always make the dog heel on the same side. If a dog tries to keep in front of you instead of walking at your side, try whirling a chain or rope in front of you as you walk. After a couple of raps on the nose he'll stay in place.

Kennel Up—A very important command for gun dogs, this means to enter anything—whether kennel, dog crate, truck, or blind. Give the command *Kennel Up* and help the dog into the crate or truck. Repeat the command, helping him until he can manage on his own.

to the next—kennel, boat, and so on. One thing you'll never have to teach an enthusiastic water dog is how to leave the car, boat, or blind!

Gun Training

Any gun dog can become gun-shy if this facet of training is not approached properly. The trick is to start out with small doses of training that are gradually increased. Some trainers recommend shooting cap pistols, then blank revolvers, and finally shotguns while the young dogs are eating. I prefer to take the dog into the field and let him (or her) run and romp. I then start shooting a cap pistol and throwing a dummy. The dog soon associates the sound with the fun of retrieving; eventually I work up to a shotgun. Once a dog becomes gun-shy, it is almost impossible to break him of this fear.

Advanced Retrieving

The next step is to teach the dog advanced retrieving. Here he learns how to interpret hand signals, and how to mark ducks and bring them to hand properly and promptly. All the first retrieving lessons should be done on land; then when the dog is working properly he can be introduced to retrieving dummies from the water.

You should start by teaching basic retrieving—something which the dog will probably already be doing eagerly on his own. But the point is that he must learn to retrieve when you want him to, and correctly. Command the dog to STAY and standing by his side give the command MARK, at the same time throwing a training dummy up and away from him. Make sure he stays at your side and sees the dummy as it is thrown, as well as where it lands. Issue the command GO or FETCH (whichever you prefer to use) and push him toward the dummy.

When the dog picks up the dummy, issue the command COME. Some gunners also like to blow a whistle at this point. Make sure the dog brings the dummy all the way back to you, then command him to SIT. Take the dummy from his mouth, thank him and praise him for a job well done. If he drops the dummy before you can take it, put it back in his mouth and hold it there until you give the command RELEASE. Then take the dummy from his mouth. The next step is to throw two dummies, and make him bring each one back to you. This is a harder lesson; it normally takes a great deal of patience and practice before the dog can bring back both dummies quickly and properly.

Once you've trained your retriever to bring dummies into hand, the next step is to train him with a real bird. Use a pigeon at first; then when the dog gets used to working with live game, bring in a tame mallard whose wings have been shackled or clipped.

After your dog has mastered retrieving, you must teach him to obey hand signals. When this is done, you'll have a complete retriever—one who can be directed to retrieve birds he didn't even see fall.

Make the dog SIT. Give him the command to MARK. Throw the training dummy past him and wave your hand at it, giving the command BACK. This way he'll learn to associate the hand wave with the idea of turning and going behind to something he can't even see. After he has learned this lesson completely, do the same type of exercise, but this time throw the dummy to one side of him and then to the other, waving your hand to direct him. Use an exaggerated hand wave to make sure he understands, and don't at any time let him rush the dummy when you throw it. Make him sit until given the command to FETCH.

Now it is time to introduce your water dog to all the phases of the sport you and he plan to enjoy together. Teach him the difference between the decoys and real ducks. Put the dog in your boat and let him get used to the movement of the water and the confinement. Later in the season when the weather becomes cold and rough, this training can really pay off. Make sure you teach the dog how and where to jump out of your boat, and how and where you want him to come back in.

Finally, there are several good books on training retrievers that go into more detail than is possible here. If you do decide to train your own water dog, I suggest you choose a couple of these from your nearest bookstore. The cost is nothing compared to the value of having your dog well trained, and you will really have an enjoyable companion for water-fowling.

DOG CARE

The work of a water dog is strenuous. Your dog should get proper care if you expect him (or her) to work well and be a happy, enthusiastic companion. Make sure he has all his immunization shots each year and is wormed. It's not a bad idea to have your dog given a physical before each hunting season.

Dogs should be fed properly. There is some controversy about whether to give a dog wet or dry foods, and whether to allow him table scraps. I think it best to follow the rule used by most trainers and choose dry dog food. The better dry foods are not only extremely well balanced but also give the dog the opportunity to chew, which helps keep the teeth

ADVANCED LAND RETRIEVING

After obedience school, "high school" begins. Give the dog the command to *Stay* . . .

Issue the command *Mark* and throw the dummy, making sure the dog stays at your side and is watching the thrown dummy . . .

Issue the command *Go* or *Fetch* and send the dog on his way with a hand signal.

When the dog picks up the training dummy, blow your whistle and give the command *Come*.

Make your dog bring the dummy back to you and sit . . .

Then take the dummy from the dog, patting him and thanking him for a job well done.

The next move is to throw two dummies. Make the dog mark both and then retrieve each.

After the dog has learned these lessons on land, repeat with the training dummy on water.

Now use a tame duck whose wings have been clipped.

HAND SIGNALS

After learning basic retrieving, the dog goes to "college" and learns hand signals. Make the dog sit, give the command to *Mark*.

Then throw the dummy past the dog, issue the command *Back,* and wave your hand back. The dog will learn to associate your arm wave with going back after something he cannot see.

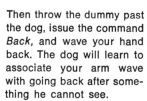

In the final step, make the dog sit, then throw to either side and send him on his way with a direct hand signal.

Nothing beats water training, and a dull bluebird afternoon can sometimes be put to advantage by refreshing your dogs on their signals, simulating the real thing.

A well-trained water dog makes a hunt even more enjoyable; and when you've successfully trained a dog by yourself, he (or she) becomes an even more valuable companion.

in good shape. Always provide plenty of clean drinking water. As for table scraps, use them only as a supplement to your dog's regular diet; be careful not to put in chicken bones or other potentially harmful scraps.

A dog that has been confined to the kennel or a limited run for a number of months should have the opportunity to unlimber his summer-soft muscles and develop his stamina before being asked for a hard day's hunt.

Starting at least a full month before actual hunting begins, you should give the dog a run of 15 to 20 minutes a day, stretched out to an hour or two on weekends. This is really all he needs to get in shape and harden up his pads for the tougher trekking ahead.

This is also the best time to reestablish the dog's quick response to basic obedience commands; 10 minutes a day is enough for this phase of preparation, but it is important. A dog that won't respond properly in the field can be more of a hindrance than a help.

While you don't want a fat field dog, remember to adjust the dog's diet to his increased activity. A good hunting dog should be slim but not starved—colder weather alone will increase his fuel requirements. You can help meet this need by adding a tablespoon or two of lard to the dog's daily winter ration. But if the dog has picked up some summer suet of his own, let him run this off before increasing the feed.

Finally, remember to match the demands on your dog to his age. Veteran dogs are much like veteran hunters. They still have the desire and enthusiasm, and a fund of experience, but their work sessions have to be paced carefully, with judicious resting periods in between. Work your dog right and his savvy will complement his staying power.

♂

♀

10

Clothing and Accessories

When it comes to duck or goose hunting, clothes do make the man. The number one rule is to wear dull clothing. Almost anything goes as long as it's dark green or some shade of brown or tan. The second rule is to keep warm and dry. There just isn't any way you can concentrate on your shooting when you're cold and wet, and with today's new outdoor gear there is no longer any reason for modern waterfowlers to be uncomfortable.

BASIC CLOTHING

Layering

During a day of duck or goose hunting, the weather may change several times; I've learned to hope for the worst and go prepared for it. The best method for keeping warm, and even more important, dry, is to wear several layers of clothing. Different layers, if chosen and worn properly, hold in body heat yet allow perspiration to escape from your body.

Having good equipment and wearing proper clothing can mean the difference between a miserable day spent afield and a pleasant, comfortable trip.

Trapped body moisture is the culprit in many cases of chilling and can even cause death. Also, if you have to slog through miles of marsh to get to your blind, no matter how cold it is, you'll be sweating under your clothes. Then you will probably climb into the blind and sit for several hours without moving. This is a very good way of getting thoroughly and dangerously chilled. The solution is to take off your outer layers of clothing and carry them to the blind. When you get to the blind, put on the outer clothing before you start to feel the cold.

After many years hunting, fishing, and running traplines in all kinds of weather, as well as living on a farm (which often means spending all day outdoors working in the worst weather to tend stock), I came up with a formula for clothing that keeps me warm and dry. This is a personal preference; each individual will have to experiment to find what kind of clothing combination keeps him warm while still allowing him to function properly during extremely cold weather.

I always wear two pairs of good wool socks. I also keep an extra pair stuck in a shell vest, coat, or ammo box. If I do a lot of walking in waders, my feet become soaked with perspiration, and I change my socks as soon as my feet start feeling clammy and cold. I've found that if I can keep my feet warm and dry, the rest of me feels much warmer and drier. Next I pull on the bottom half of a suit of thermal underwear. If you can't wear wool underwear, a good substitute is a set of the fishnet type. Instead of the top half of the underwear suit, I prefer a turtleneck sweater; one made of wool and nylon not only keeps my upper torso warm but my neck as well. A very important feature for a winter shirt, but particularly an undershirt, is a long tail so the shirt will stay tucked in and not allow any cold drafts around your back.

Over this I wear a heavy wool shirt. Because I couldn't buy wool shirts that fit snugly yet allowed freedom in the arms for good shooting, my wife started making my shirts. We have discovered that the new wool-acrylic materials are just as effective as all wool in keeping you dry and warm, and can be laundered in the automatic washer without any ill effects.

I don't like to wear the bottom half of hunting suits. I find these pants just too heavy to lug around, and unless they've been broken in for ten years, they are too stiff and uncomfortable to sit in. Instead, I like to wear a good pair of jeans. They're comfortable to walk and sit in, and not only keep out the cold but allow your body moisture to escape. The trick in buying jeans for cold weather wear is to buy them one size larger than you would during warmer weather. This allows for the extra clothes underneath and for comfort when you're sitting in a blind.

On mild days I wear an ordinary game shell vest over the shirt and a camouflage cap. When the weather starts getting colder, I slip a down vest under the shell vest. These layers of clothing keep me plenty warm in everything but the severest cold; then I usually add a wool hunting coat, and over that a waterproof rain jacket with hood in a camouflage pattern.

ADDITIONAL GEAR

Raingear

Waterfowling and wet weather go together, so I always carry good raingear. Many cheap kinds of raingear are made of heavy canvas and rubber and are so ponderous you can hardly walk in them. Their main problem, however, is that they not only keep all the rain out but also have no ventilation areas to allow moisture to escape from inside. You become just as clammy and wet as if you hadn't worn a suit at all. When purchas-

Fishnet underwear is a good choice for those who can't wear wool.

A good hunting coat in a camouflage pattern can help conceal the hunter, as well as keep him warm and dry.

Hunters who like to work small potholes or flooded timber would appreciate this combined camouflage-poncho and decoy carrier.

When the weather really gets cold and rough, slip into a subzero suit.

ing a rain suit, always buy the best, preferably a lightweight suit made of rip-proof nylon.

Hip Waders

Some duck hunters seem to get by with hip waders, but not me! If I'm in a duck pond guaranteed to be not over 2 feet deep, somehow I'll stumble into a hole big enough for a truck. A couple of years ago I would have given a perfectly good set of hip waders to the first person who offered me a cup of hot coffee. A friend and I were hunting on a public lake in Kansas, and the first thing I did when we started out to the blind was to catch my foot on a sunken log and stumble enough to fill both hip waders with icy water. Just about that time a rustling of wings announced a large flight of ducks bearing down on us low and fast, and as

A good rain suit consisting of pants and parka can save the day. Wearing rain ponchos, or raincoats without rain pants, allows all the water to run down the back of your legs.

For light duty and shallow wading, many hunters like hip waders.

the sun began to peep over the treetops, I could see the gray sky filled with ducks trading back and forth. Our blind was only 100 yards away, so we continued while I issued a few choice words about hip waders and duck hunting in general. We broke the skim ice around our decoys and crawled into our blind. Naturally, we saw more ducks that morning than we had all season; after about two hours of hot gunning and cold feet, I finally headed back to the car. My buddy went home, and I went straight to the sporting goods store.

If you're shooting for field birds and you're sure you won't be crossing any ditches, the best footwear may be knee-high rubber boots. But again, I somehow always manage to find a ditch to cross, and so I usually wear lightweight hip waders for field hunting geese and ducks.

Chest Waders

Choosing chest waders is much like choosing raingear. Pick only the best—because they're not only your defense against the cold and wet, but protection for your life as well. Insulated waders are well worth the extra price if your duck and goose hunting is done in extremely cold climates.

It's not a bad idea to test your new waders out in the bathtub before you take off on an icy morning duck hunt. Even new waders can have small pinhole leaks that will allow enough water in to make you uncomfortable.

Chestwaders can be much more dangerous than hip waders if you get into deep water with them. However, if worn properly, they can also save your life in deep water.

A good friend of mine walked off into a deep creek channel running through a supposedly shallow duck lake and ended up over his head. As he dropped out of sight, he shot up the hand that was holding his gun over his head, and we started looking for something to pull him out with. His chest waders had filled with water and sunk him to the bottom. He knew we were only about 20 feet from him on the opposite bank, and lucky he kept his head. He calmly walked on the bottom until he reached us, carefully holding his gun out of the water all the time. When we dragged him ashore, he was a pretty tuckered out but mighty relieved duck hunter!

From that day on, both he and I wore a tight belt around the top portion of our waders. If you go into deep water with waders fixed in this way, the air trapped in the waders will float your feet to the surface. All you have to do is keep your head and swim your way out.

In an emergency situation—a swamped boat in deep water far from shore, for instance—you can also remove the waders, turn them upside

I prefer insulated chest waders for all my waterfowling except early season hunts. The extra height keeps your feet dry should you step into a hole—and your seat dry when you settle on a frosted early morning blind.

A good safety measure is to wear a belt clasped tightly around your middle and over the waders. It traps air in the waders, which will help you float should you step into deep water.

down, and use them as a float to keep you up in the water. I wear a sheath knife on the belt, where it too can be reached quickly and easily in an emergency.

Handwarmers

One of the most indispensable items for cold weather hunting is a good handwarmer, or even two. A great new product is a body belt, worn around your middle, that is especially designed so that it will hold two handwarmers, giving you that extra bit of warmth that will keep you happy all day. I have one of the large-size handwarmers, which I always fill at the beginning of each day; it will usually last the entire day.

Gloves

If you are one of those unfortunate individuals who just can't seem to shoot with gloves (as I am), you have to keep your hands in your

One of the best pieces of equipment for the outdoorsman venturing into the cold is a handwarmer.

A body belt that holds two handwarmers and is worn around your middle section can help keep your entire body warm.

pockets or near a handwarmer until you need them for calling or shooting. However, I have found that the large waterproof gloves used by professional trappers are excellent for handling wet decoys in icy water.

If you need to wear gloves, there are several kinds of shooting gloves that can be worn in cold and wet weather and still enable you to shoot. When it gets bitter cold, I do use gloves—two layers, in fact, a common pair of wool driving gloves under a larger pair of waterproof gloves.

One item that could be great for waterfowling is the new snowmobile suit. Unfortunately, most of the suits are manufactured with fashion in mind and are brightly colored. When some manufacturer starts producing them in camouflage colors, you're sure to see a rush to the sporting goods stores by knowledgeable outdoorsmen.

Backpack

Yes, I use a small backpack when duck hunting. Many of the places I hunt require a mile or so of walking to get to the blind, often crossing sloughs, ditches, and marshes. Trying to carry a vacuum bottle, shells, gun, camera, lunch, and decoys without dropping something in the mud and water can get to be quite a problem, so I started putting everything into a small backpack. The pack is a two-piece outfit, consisting of an aluminum frame and dark green nylon pack bag. It enables me to carry a bit more than otherwise and can be stood in the mud of a blind bottom, keeping all my things high and dry. The individual pockets make items easy to locate and grab in a hurry.

About a year ago my wife and I were doing some goose hunting on a

Nothing beats the frogman-style gloves for putting out and picking up "dekes" in icy water. They are often used by trappers for deploying water sets.

These camouflaged shooting mittens keep your hands warm and dry, while enabling you to remove your fingers quickly for shooting or reloading.

A good backpack may get you a little ribbing from your buddies, but more than makes up in the comfortable way you can carry goodies to the blind.

private reserve near Swan Lake. We knew we would have to walk over a mile across a muddy soybean field. When we prepared to leave our car in the morning, many of the other hunters were a little startled to see me shoulder a backpack, and I got a good bit of ribbing. But we got the last laugh! With everything we needed, we were able to stay in the goose pit all day, collect our limit of geese, take a beautiful collection of color pictures with the several cameras and rolls of film I had carried, and enjoy a gourmet lunch complete with napkins and all the trimmings.

Caps

Headgear is especially important in waterfowling for several reasons. The first is to keep your head warm and dry. I personally prefer to wear one of the lighter weight camouflage caps and pull up the hood of my raingear if the weather gets bad; but in extreme cold the best headgear is a wool stocking or watch cap that can be pulled far down over your ears and around your face. The hood of your camouflage coat can then be pulled down over the cap.

The second reason for wearing a cap is to hide part of your face from the ducks. Sometime when you're not too far from another blind of hunters, watch them closely. No matter how well the blind is concealed or the hunters are camouflaged in clothing, you can spot a white face as soon as one of them moves. I know one hunter who hunts exclusively on public hunting areas, and he believes one of the reasons he is successful is that he wears full head camouflage just as he does when hunting wild turkeys.

If you wear glasses it is a good idea to wear a cap with a long bill, again to cut down the chances of a sudden flash of light or reflection flaring ducks from your blind.

Miscellaneous Accessories

Waterfowlers aren't quite as gadget-minded as some other hunters and fishermen, but there are still several items that can really make a hunt more enjoyable.

Much waterfowling is done over a fairly long period of time. Often waterfowlers rise way before dawn and stay in the marsh until the sun goes down. Food is one of the major concerns. I always carry a vacuum bottle of coffee and one of soup. I also take a small plastic bag of home-made deer jerky and one of hard candy. All this doesn't weigh very much, yet it provides me with a variety of tastes and can keep me going all day.

I carry a small flashlight for finding my way to the blind in the hours before daylight, and a large belt knife for cutting extra camouflage materials for the blind.

When hunting large open waters, I like to take along a small, light-weight pair of binoculars. They are small enough to slip into a pocket, yet strong enough for spotting ducks trading on the distant lakeshores. When the shooting gets slow and "boring," the binoculars are invaluable for studying the other wildlife activity going on around the blind.

If your blind is accessible by auto or boat or you're shooting from a boat, there are several accessories that can make your day more pleasant. A catalytic heater in a boat or blind can keep you comfortable all day, even with a sleet storm howling outside. One caution: These units emit carbon monoxide and duck hunters have been killed using them in tight, unventilated blinds.

Another handy accessory is an army surplus ammo box to carry shells, camera, food, glasses, or almost any breakable or perishable item. Even if set down in the mud of a blind floor, it will keep the items dry and safe.

Of course, one of the handiest pieces of equipment for the water-fowler is a four-wheel-drive vehicle. The more inaccessible a duck blind or marsh, the better it is, particularly if you are renting or leasing a blind or lake, otherwise you'll have problems with road hunters and poachers. The only solution for many hunters is to lease a blind or lake in a place that is almost inaccessible and then buy a four-wheel-drive vehicle to get to it. Granted this is a big investment; but by the same token, today's well-engineered four-wheel-drive vehicles can be as fancy or as practical as your family car. Many sportsmen have found them excellent as second vehicles; they can be used to great advantage for hauling decoys, dogs, and gear to a secret hunting spot, yet they can also ferry the kids, fetch the groceries, or even drive grandmother to church.

Four-wheel-drive vehicles can get stuck, however; and if you finally do hang one up, you'll really have a job on your hands. Anyone who does much off-road traveling, especially in mucky marshland, should keep an electric winch on the front of the vehicle.

There are a few common mistakes made by hunters when driving bad roads like the ones found near duck and goose hunting country. One is waiting until it's too late before shifting into four-wheel drive; another is misjudging your vehicle's load. Even a four-wheel drive won't handle as well if the back end, particularly the station-wagon-type, is empty. A

One "accessory" almost considered a necessity by many waterfowlers is a 4-wheel-drive vehicle for getting back into the rough country where the hunting is good.

good method used by many farmers is to keep a couple of 100 pound bags of sand over each rear wheel even in four-wheel-drive pickups. They give a lot more traction to the rear wheels. A further problem with a four-wheel drive is high centering. If the road is deeply rutted, it's often better to stay off it, otherwise you stand a chance of slipping off into the deep ruts and high-centering your vehicle. Of course, if you're driving across a dike, you must stay on the road.

One of the best tricks to "mud" driving is to get out of your vehicle, examine the area, and try to pick the best route. Then get up enough speed to carry you through while still holding you on your sighted route.

♂

♀

11

Dressing and Cooking Waterfowl

You've had a beautiful day of shooting. Beside you in the blind lies a brace of corn-fed greenheads. As you pick them up and start lugging your gear back to your car, you think of the hour's drive home, putting all the gear away—and you've still got to dress those blasted ducks! Unfortunately, this is where many hunters give up. Plucking ducks and geese does involve some work, but the results if prepared properly will be a feast that even your gourmet friends will envy. Waterfowl have traditionally been the food of kings and lords, and with a little effort you too can enjoy those excellent table birds. With the rising cost of meat, waterfowl will be a welcome addition to your table.

I learned the illustrated method of dressing water birds from a professional duck guide who dresses hundreds each year. It is a quick and easy method, involving 5 to 10 minutes a duck. If you belong to a duck club or dress a great number of ducks or geese, you may wish to invest in a duck plucker. These machines can pick a duck or goose clean of all feathers and down in a matter of minutes.

Ducks and geese should be well wrapped for freezing, preferably with a double layer. Wrap first with a plastic wrap, then with a good

If you pluck a large number of ducks, you may wish to buy a duck plucker. These handy machines make short work of a tedious chore.

Many sportsmen save the down from geese for pillows, jackets, or sleeping bags. First clean and age the down by the Indian method of hanging it outside all winter in a bag. The down will be washed by the rain, dried by the sun, and fluffed by the wind, and the freezing will kill all lice and other vermin.

waxed freezer paper, double-folding the edges and taping with freezer tape. Or the ducks can be immersed in water and frozen in milk cartons. Well-wrapped ducks and geese will keep in the freezer for about nine months.

Goose and duck down was used by old-timers to make pillows and mattresses, and today hunters can still use it to make vests, sleeping bags, and so on. The trick is to clean the down of lice and dirt. One method

A pair of corn-fed mallards will make a meal fine enough to grace any table. But they must be properly cared for from the moment they're shot to the moment they're served.

Some of the finest eating in the world comes from these small but delicious blue-winged teal. You will need about two ducks a person, but they're worth the effort.

DRESSING A DUCK

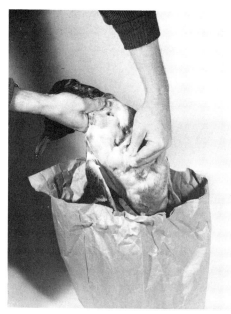

The real key to easy plucking is to dry-pick downward. Start at the breast and always pick downward. Pick the duck as quickly as possible after killing, and the feathers will release more easily. Picking over a paper bag keeps the feathers from flying all over and makes for easy cleanup.

Cut around the wing socket with a sharp knife.

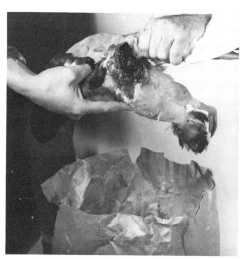

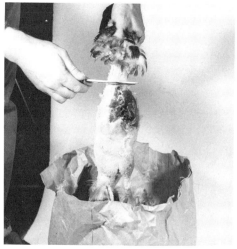

Bend the wing bone out of its socket. You may have to cut some muscle here to release the wing.

With a sharp knife, cut off the head and feet.

Cut off the tail.

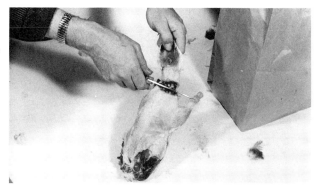

For easier preparing and cooking of ducks, remove backbone. Start cutting at the base of the tail as shown.

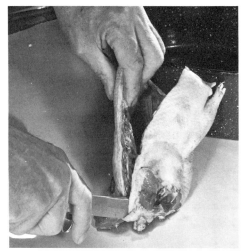

Cut through the ribs and down the side of the neck.

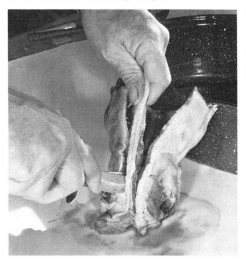

Make a cut down the opposite side of the backbone as shown.

Remove the backbone, neck, and entrails. Wash out the cavity, and put the duck in a plastic bag for freezing.

used by the Indians is to hang the down outside in bags over the winter. The constant rain, wind, and sun cleans the down, making it fresh and sweet-smelling.

After picking and cleaning the duck or goose, place it in a pan of cold salt water (about ½ cup salt to 1 quart of water) and leave it in the refrigerator overnight. One of the prime necessities when preparing any game bird is to make sure you remove all damaged flesh around shot holes. Remove all blood and bloody tissue by first soaking in salt water and then cutting bad spots away.

I'm not going to try to tell you that ducks don't taste like wild meat. They taste like wild ducks and geese! Unfortunately, many people have never tasted wild game that has been properly cared for and cooked, and they have prejudices against almost any wild game, especially dark-meated fowl like ducks and geese. But if prepared correctly and given all the attention they deserve, both ducks and geese can provide some exquisite eating.

Ducks have a particularly dry meat, and all efforts should be made to seal in the natural juices. Adding fat from pieces of bacon can make the meat juicier and cut down on some of the wild taste. Because of their dryness, ducks should never be overcooked; they become powdery and tasteless. Duck meat should be just a bit on the rare side. Ducks are done if the juices are no longer red when pricked with a fork or the meat between the leg and body is a faint pink.

Stuffing the birds with apples, onions, celery, raisins, and oranges will also remove some of the gamey taste. The stuffing, however, is usually discarded. If you like the rich wild taste of goose, use a bread stuffing just as you would for a young turkey and wait for some mouth-watering food.

Knowing the age of the duck or goose can help you determine how you're going to prepare it. It takes a bit more time in marinating and cooking to tenderize an older bird than it does a first-year fowl. Cooking approximately 20 to 30 minutes per pound at 325° oven should tenderize about the toughest of birds, while a higher oven (about 375–400°) and a somewhat shorter cooking time should be sufficient for a young bird.

All fish-eating ducks should be marinated and cooked on a rack so their fat, which holds much of the fishy taste, is drained away. The cooking juices of these ducks should never be used in sauces or gravies. Spicy recipes will also help to cover some of the fish taste. A good simple marinade is equal parts dry red wine and water, salt, pepper. Then add whatever spices your family likes—onions, garlic, dry mustard, celery salt, Tabasco, soy and Worcestershire sauce are all good with ducks.

Parboiling ducks and geese will help remove the gamey taste, especially from fish-eating ducks. Cover ducks with water and add a quartered apple, onion and/or a stalk of celery to the water. Simmer about 15 to 20 minutes, remove duck, and finish cooking in your favorite way.

Ducks and geese are normally cooked on a stove or in the oven, but they can also provide some truly great eating if cooked outside over charcoal or an open campfire. They may be cooked on a spit over a low fire, basted frequently with either a barbecue sauce or a butter-based herb sauce; 20 to 25 minutes on a spit and about 12 minutes on a grill (ducks split down back) should cook a medium-sized duck. Decrease the time somewhat for teal and double the time for geese.

Ducks and geese and a very similar bird, the dove, are great wrapped with a piece of bacon, stuffed with apples and onions, wrapped in foil, and baked over an open or charcoal fire. The fire should be quite low, and the birds should be turned frequently. This recipe takes about 1 hour for a medium-sized duck on a very low fire.

Ducks may be halved, just like a chicken, or the breasts may be removed and cooked over a charcoal fire with frequent basting. This method using halved ducks should take about 30 minutes for a medium-sized duck on a medium fire.

One great way of cooking small ducks such as teal is to place them in a deep saucepan and cover with a wine sauce. Cook until the meat falls from the bones, and you will have the juiciest, sweetest-tasting duck ever.

I also like duck roasted, then served cold on toast with a piece of lettuce and lots of horseradish.

These are some of my favorite recipes for preparing ducks and geese.

Roast Ducks and Wild Rice

Clean two ducks and soak overnight in salt water.

Fry several bacon slices to melt the fat. Remove the bacon strips, and prepare a rather thin flour-and-water gravy, since this will thicken as it bakes. Add 1 cup dry red wine to the gravy. Salt and pepper the inside and outside of the ducks, and add onions and apples to the chest cavity. Place ducks in a roaster breast side up and pour gravy over them. Lay additional bacon strips across any exposed breast skin. Place a tight lid on pan, and bake in a 325° oven for about 2 hours.

Serve over wild rice.

Fried Duck or Goose

For a quick meal of duck or goose, remove the breast meat and cut across the grain in ¼-inch slices. Pound slices of meat to tenderize, dredge with salt, pepper, and flour. Fry in hot fat for just a few minutes.

Make gravy from the drippings.

Cold Duck Sandwiches

Serve breast meat sliced thin on bread that has been spread with mayonnaise and horseradish.

Duck Pâté

Stew cleaned ducks until meat falls from bones. This could also be carcasses from which the breast was used or leftover cooked meat.

Debone meat and grind. Moisten lightly with mayonnaise and horseradish. Serve on small sandwiches or with crackers.

Roast Goose and Dressing

Clean and marinate two geese in salt water overnight. Salt and pepper geese inside and out, and fill cavities with quartered onions. Put geese on rack in roasting pan and cover chests with bacon strips or rub with butter. Add 1 cup dry red wine and water to roaster to a depth of about 2 inches. Bake at 325° about 2 hours or until meat between leg and body is a delicate pink. When geese are done, remove from pan and carve. Make gravy—dicing gizzard and liver into it—from half the broth; save other half to moisten dressing.

DRESSING

In a large bowl break up equal amounts of day-old white bread and yellow cornbread. Add salt, pepper, and sage or poultry seasoning to taste. Moisten with eggs (four to six to a gallon bowl) and broth. Bake in hot oven until set.

Creamed Duck or Goose

All leftover meat and all carcasses cooked or uncooked are put in a pot and covered with water. Simmer for an hour or two until all meat falls off the bones. Strain the broth and return all meat to it. Thicken slightly with cornstarch or flour and water, and serve over noodles, rice, or hot biscuits.

Campfire Ducks (*from Doradee Kelso*)

Bone breast of duck and divide into two equal parts. Marinate in enough soy sauce to cover meat about ½ hour. Place on rack or spit and cook over hot coals, turning frequently until done (about ½ hour). Return to reserved soy sauce and cook about 10 minutes. Slice and serve.

Buttered Ducks (*from Ed Dobbins*)

Into cavity of each duck place one stalk of celery and half an apple. Salt, pepper, and flour. Place breast down in ½-inch of water. Butter back of ducks. Roast uncovered in preheated 400° oven for 20 minutes. Lower oven to 250° for 90 minutes. Turn ducks breast side up and baste with butter for about 30 minutes.

Orange Stuffing (*from Ed Dobbins*)

3 cups toasted bread cubes	2 cups diced celery
1½ cups hot water	¼ cup melted butter
2 teaspoons grated orange rind	1 beaten egg
⅔ cups orange pulp	½ teaspoon salt; pepper to taste

Soak bread cubes in hot water for 15 minutes. Add other ingredients. Mix well and stuff loosely in ducks.

Orange Ducks (*from Bill Thomas*)

Rub onion, salt, and garlic on body and cavity of ducks. For each duck mix one diced apple and one small box of raisins—place in cavity. Set ducks in pan containing ½ inch orange juice and cook 2 hours at 325°. Baste often. Remove from oven and take meat off bones. Replace in same pan with cooking juices and cook another 20 minutes at 325°. Drain and serve. Cooked apples, raisins, and juice may be mixed and served as a side dish.

♀

♂

12

Waterfowl Conservation

Do you think your children will be able to enjoy the excitement of a day spent hunting waterfowl? Well, it's up to you and me to make sure they will, for each of us has a very important stake in the future of waterfowl and a role to play in its preservation.

The greatest single threat to waterfowl is our booming population. Ducks and geese need lots of room, and unfortunately their food and habitat requirements are in direct conflict with today's land use. Our growing population demands more grain and more efficient use of the land, and this has caused millions of acres of prairie pothole country—the traditional nesting grounds of 65 percent of all North American waterfowl—to be drained and converted from wetlands to agricultural use. By the same token, we have drained millions of coastal marshes for suburban housing developments, freeways, and sprawling airports.

In the Midwestern states we have dammed up the vital rivers, changing their bottomlands from ideal duck habitat to useless non-food-producing lakes and mudflats. On the other hand, the present inefficient system of grain cropping has left tons of waste grain in the fields, and the more adaptable birds such as mallards and geese have learned to seek

A family of Canada geese swims slowly across the waters of a restored wetland in a national refuge.

out this waste. When we learn more efficient means of harvesting, which of course we must do, and we start plowing crop residues under right after harvest, this source of food for waterfowl will also be gone.

POPULATION

As we learned at the beginning of this century, the only way man and wild animals and birds can live together on this planet is with sound game management.

In general, a habitat can be managed with care and intelligence so that an increase in its bird and animal population is brought about. Waterfowl, however, present particularly complex problems in management. They are great travelers, and in the course of one year a North American duck or goose will travel literally millions of miles across three countries in search of places to nest, eat, and spend the winter. Additionally, each species has its own individual requirements and poses different questions.

As a result of these wide-ranging activities and specific needs, waterfowl are constantly on a boom-and-bust population. A dry year in Canada may cause a drastic decrease in nesting success, which in turn will affect waterfowl that eventually winter in Mexico. A sudden loss of valuable wintering grounds in our Southern coastal states due to development, or changing land use, may mean starvation to millions of waterfowl that have depended on the area for generations.

Because such a great deal of waterfowl habitat has already been converted into lands unsuitable for waterfowl, game managers have been forced to realize that there is no way to bring the waterfowl populations back to what they were at the first part of the century. However, waterfowl biologists think that with the correct controls we can eventually bring the population back to the high level of the early 1950s and prevent the huge bust of the early 1960s.

WEATHER

With fewer and fewer places to nest, many birds are forced into areas they wouldn't normally use, and their chances for survival there are not always good. The "duck factory," or northern prairie pothole country, is actually semi-arid country. It averages less than 20 inches of rainfall each year, and nesting success depends on whether the yearly spring and early summer rainfall comes in time to fill the potholes for the arrival of breeding birds. Many waterfowl will try for a second nesting if they are foiled in the first attempt. But if they are too far north they may not get a second chance, or their young may be too small and weak at the time of the fall migration.

Plenty of food and shelter are essential in waterfowl wintering grounds.

Too much water, unusual cold spells, hail, or storms in nesting areas, are other hazards that might destroy young birds. Wintering grounds have to provide weary travelers with plenty of food and resting space, and freak storms in these areas can sometimes cause the loss of both.

DISEASE

Disease, particularly botulism and fowl cholera, takes a heavy toll on waterfowl. During warm weather, botulism is a particularly bad problem in the Western United States. Although the number of waterfowl that die each year from this disease is relatively small, there is always the possibility of an epidemic in heavy concentrations of waterfowl.

PREDATORS

Waterfowl and marsh animals are vital to each other and to their habitat. Many marsh dwellers may be predators of ducks, especially ducklings or eggs. But predators are nature's way of keeping a species in

Predators, like this raccoon, are a natural threat to waterfowl, especially to young and the eggs of nesting hens.

Another problem in waterfowl management is controlling the animals that compete directly with waterfowl for food, for instance, this muskrat.

balance; only when nesting birds are more concentrated than normal, resulting in over-predation, is there any need for control.

Other animals compete with ducks for habitat. For example, musk-rats and ducks seem to go together, and when you find good habitat for one, you will often find the other. If muskrats overpopulate an area, they can become a serious problem. They compete directly with ducks for food, and in some areas become so concentrated they literally eat the ducks out of food. This problem has occurred in Louisiana, Oregon, Minnesota, and New Jersey.

The present decline in fur trapping is already increasing the number of fur animals in the marshes, and this causes an even greater competition for habitat.

LEAD

One of the most hotly argued problems in management today concerns birds dying from ingesting spent lead shot. Although this problem is common only in areas with relatively hard-bottomed wetlands where shot does not sink quickly, it does kill an estimated 1 to 2 percent of the ducks that migrate into and through the United States each fall.

For the past several years, the ammunition industry has devoted much effort to finding a nontoxic substitute for lead, even though it is recognized that it will take many years for the shot now present in affected areas to disappear. Extensive research has shown the most promising material to be steel (iron). But aside from its advantages, steel (iron) shot still raises a number of questions. Among these are:

1. Is it as effective as lead or does it result in more crippling losses?
2. Is it safe for both guns and shooters?
3. Will it be more expensive than lead?
4. Does it damage barrels and chokes?
5. If it proves to be less effective and more expensive than lead, what kind of regulations will be needed for its use?

During the 1971–72 waterfowl season, in an effort to find answers to some of these questions, Remington Arms Company, Inc., conducted tests on experimental twelve-gauge shotgun shells loaded with steel shot. These tests were conducted under actual hunting conditions at Remington Farm—the company's wildlife management demonstration area, located near Chestertown, Maryland.

All guests at the farm were asked to do half of their duck hunting with steel and the remainder with lead shot. The days on which each type of shot was to be used were set up in advance, and records were kept on weather conditions, actual numbers of rounds fired, total birds bagged with each type, ranges at which birds were shot, and comparative numbers of cripples versus clean kills. In addition, the guns were checked daily to determine the effects of steel shot on the barrels.

The experimental shells were loaded with 1⅛ ounces of no. 4 steel shot. The control shells were conventional Remington Express loads, with no. 6 lead loads. Previous tests had shown that no. 4 steel shot gives a ballistic performance comparable to no. 6 lead.

The results of the test indicate that at ranges up to 35 yards, 1⅛ no. 4 steel loads are only slightly less effective for duck hunting than 1¼ no. 6 lead loads. However, at ranges greater than 35 yards, the steel loads appear to cause more crippling than the lead.

This problem merits extremely careful study and research. Unfortunately, it is also an emotional one, and steel shot is in danger of being forced into the waterfowlers' hands by political maneuvers without the necessary testing.

LOSS OF HABITAT

Wetlands provide habitat for hundreds of species of waterfowl, animals, and small birds. Year by year, however, the wetlands are gradually disappearing. We are converting them into land for planting wheat and corn, and for building houses, roads, airports, and factories. It is only recently that we have begun to consider the wetlands' importance. Of the estimated 127 million acres of wetlands that existed during colonial times in the United States, more than 45 million acres have been converted to other uses.

If we want to continue to see any waterfowl, we must do something about this gradual disappearance of our wetlands and ensure proper management of those that still exist and are suitable for waterfowl.

One of the largest problem areas is the Canadian provinces of Manitoba, Saskatchewan, and Alberta, where most North American ducks begin their lives. This fertile country is very important agriculturally; as a result, millions of acres of marshes and prairie potholes have been drained and filled to provide land for more farming and grazing. The coastal United States presents another problem—here wetlands are lost through the diking of marshlands.

Throughout the United States, prime duck habitat has been drained or inundated by flood-control reservoirs. Already over 9 million acres of marsh have been ditched, channeled, and drained in the Southern coastal

Changing land use is the single most threatening danger to waterfowl as more and more wetlands are cleared for roads, shopping centers, suburban developments, etc.

One of the worst problems for the future of waterfowl is the constant draining, dredging, and channelization of streams and wetlands.

states. For example, in the Mississippi flyway many of the oxbows and marshes of vital river systems have been altered for flood control or to provide for more agricultural land or urban shopping centers.

Iowa was once a very important duck-producing state, but here too ditching and other agricultural practices have been put to popular use, reducing duck production to almost nothing.

Fortunately, we may not have reached the point of no return. The federal and state governments are purchasing wetlands and restoring them through extensive management to productive levels. However, acquiring and reclaiming wetlands is not the only answer. The majority of duck-producing wetlands are still privately owned, and programs that stress the value of these lands as wetlands (rather than as drained agricultural or development lands) are of enormous importance. Such programs often involve reimbursing the landowner for keeping and improving vital wetlands. At cross-purposes, however, are the governmental groups that are interested in the conversion of wetlands and consequently subsidize ditching and channelization.

Almost as harmful as drainage is the system of flood control based on vast reservoirs. Such reservoirs completely inundate huge river bottom valleys. If left alone, these valleys would normally flood each fall, providing migrating flights of waterfowl with plenty of food and resting places. The huge reservoirs, on the other hand, kill what bottomland food exists, flooding the valleys so deeply that there is food only for the hardy divers who can find it and fight the boating traffic.

The only reservoirs that are helpful to waterfowl are those situated near large fields of corn, millet, or milo, that are made into refuges and closed to all traffic. The ducks can then feed in the fields and rest on the open waters of the reservoirs.

A concerned waterfowler can fight this gradual eating away of vital wetlands by helping any program or organization, whether private or government, that works to restore and preserve the wetlands.

POLLUTION

Pollution is one very direct cause of waterfowl deaths. Oil pollution is a particularly serious problem in many wetlands. Spilled oil in coastal waters spells disaster for any waterfowl unlucky enough to come into contact with it. The oil mats up the birds' insulating feathers so that they quickly freeze to death in cold weather. Or they may become so covered with oil that they can't fly and eventually starve to death. The oil causes

One task of waterfowl management in federal and state refuges is providing food. This cornfield has been cropped on a shares agreement with a neighboring farmer.

the down and other feathers to lose their buoyancy, and a duck or goose may actually drown if it can't get out of the water. Birds also die from ingesting oil while attempting to preen or drink. All efforts must be made to stop oil spillage on the high seas, coastal areas, and huge riverways.

One of the underestimated dangers for waterfowl is the common oil-sludge pit (or oil sump). Ranging in size from 20 feet square to half an acre or more, these pits dot the land over the oil-producing areas of Wyoming, South Dakota, Nebraska, Kansas, and Colorado—in other words, the heart of the central flyway. To a migrating duck or goose the oil pits look like small ponds, especially inviting during dry years. The birds land, are coated with oil, and quickly die. According to the U.S. Fish and Wildlife Service, between 25,000 and 30,000 birds succumbed to the lure of these pits in Colorado in 1972.

The fact that these pits exist is even more distressing when one realizes how easy it is to clean them up. Also, there are laws against letting oil collect on the surface of these ponds. Fines can be levied, and the petroleum industry is making an effort to put its house in order. But in the meantime, waterfowl continue to land in the oil-sludge pits and die.

Other kinds of water pollution are just as serious, including the slow kinds that you don't see but that gradually deteriorate the quality of the water. Acid mining waste that leaks from dumped coal into streams and

Oil spills and oil pollution spell disaster for all kinds of waterfowl.

lakes causes all the food in the lakes to die and destroys much good wetland waterfowl habitat.

MANAGEMENT PROBLEMS

Waterfowl management is a highly complicated and sophisticated science, involving literally thousands of dedicated people and hard-earned skills and technology. Today's management includes such activities as aerial population counting, banding to determine migration routes, and even growing feed and improvising shelters. Often, conflicting interests and management practices develop between states and countries—and waterfowl suffer the consequences.

The very act of waterfowl management can cause some problems for the birds. For example, keeping birds wintering further north than they are accustomed to often causes great numbers of birds to concentrate in small areas, and the chance of epidemics increases. One such incident occurred in 1973 on the Lake Andes National Wildlife Refuge in South Dakota. Over 100,000 ducks were concentrated in a small lake that had been kept from freezing by pumping an artesian well. The duck plague took over, and within several weeks almost 29,000 ducks and 300 geese had died.

Another problem with heavy concentrations of birds in a managed area is the deterioration of surrounding cropland. This can become critical unless the refuge has enough "natural" food for the birds using the area.

Banding birds is a sophisticated management method for studying their habits, migration, life span, etc.

There is still much hope for the future of waterfowl, and with everyone's help our grandchildren and their grandchildren may know the precious heritage of waterfowling. The states alone control over 7 million acres of wetlands, managed primarily for waterfowl. Each time a hunter purchases a duck stamp, he is joining the drive to purchase, preserve, and restore marshlands. These stamps, a result of the Migratory Bird Hunting Stamp Act of 1934, are largely responsible for the close to 300 federal wildlife refuges consisting of nearly 29 million acres that are scattered across the United States. They also protect literally millions of other bird and animal species.

These refuges are a vital factor in the survival of our waterfowl because they provide food and shelter along the migratory routes. Another source of aid for acquiring and managing these gigantic marshes and wetlands are the taxes which hunters pay on guns and ammunition.

To keep up with the constant loss of habitat brought on by civilization, we must continually acquire and restore wetlands, and manage them to provide more suitable land for both birds and animals.

Hunting is still by far the most popular way in which the American public enjoys its waterfowl. One of the challenges facing today's wetland managers is to provide more space so more people can be rewarded with good hunting.

Every individual, whether hunter or no, can help preserve our waterfowl through state programs such as the Green Tree programs in Arkansas or through national organizations such as Ducks Unlimited. We can also help by fighting for legislation that will protect and preserve what waterfowl habitat we have, not only on public land but even more importantly on private land, which contains over 90 percent of today's suitable

CONSERVATION
METHODS IN USE

Providing artificial nesting sites like this old washtub positioned on a post in the water in a state refuge is another way of helping waterfowl.

"Green Tree" programs in Arkansas have restored vast wetlands areas and provided habitat for millions of mallards and pintails.

Federal refuges scattered across the United States provide food and resting areas for millions of birds.

waterfowl habitat. We can work for county, state, and national programs to rebuild marshes that have deteriorated and are no longer suitable as good waterfowl habitat.

Programs that work to build ponds, establish small marshlands, or provide irrigation ditches should not be underestimated. Even the smallest pothole may mean a nesting site for a blue-winged teal or mallard.

Much of today's waterfowl owes its existence to organizations such as Ducks Unlimited. In 1937, Ducks Unlimited was incorporated as a nonprofit membership organization dedicated to the wise conservation of waterfowl and the perpetuation of the noble heritage of waterfowling. Since the movement began three and a half decades ago, Ducks Unlimited has led the way in the protection of waterfowl, using all its facilities to restore, preserve, and create nesting habitats for ducks and geese. Ducks Unlimited has spent over $17 million to plan and develop well over 1,000 "duck factories," and has raised more than $23 million through the contributions of concerned sportsmen and organizations in the United States and Canada. All sportsmen who enjoy a day in a duck marsh should contribute to the future of waterfowl by helping such organizations as Ducks Unlimited.

Individual waterfowlers can also be a great help in restoring the waterfowl populations, not only through their dollars but by extra effort in the field. Learn to identify birds properly so no unwanted birds are wasted and limited species won't be over-shot. Respect seasons and limits —these are set by the Department of the Interior after a full year of observing the nesting season, weather, and hundreds of other factors. The seasons and limits are decided upon in a council meeting involving the department personnel, people from each of the flyways, and members of private organizations like Ducks Unlimited. After setting an initial season

The efforts of Ducks Unlimited should be supported by every waterfowler, as they are fighting most vigorously to protect and preserve wetlands. This is one of their outlet structures in Alberta, Canada. It is used to control the level of water in a gigantic marsh complex.

This is the way many people see the noble Canada goose—a good enough reason for fighting to save valuable wetlands.

and limits, each state is then allowed to establish its own within the framework set up by the Department of the Interior. This entire process is an extremely complicated one, involving a great amount of research and cooperation between the different agencies. The results are for one purpose only: *to ensure perpetuation of the species through proper cropping and management.*

Through our combined efforts, we can fight to save and restore our wetlands and prime waterfowl habitat. Through our contributions in taxes and duck stamps to seek out better management methods, we can bring back our waterfowl for everyone to enjoy, whether we thrill to an occasional glimpse of a flight of autumn Canadas winging across an autumn sky or prefer to sit in a spray-drenched blind, gunning for bluebills skimming fast and low across the waves.

♂

♀

13

Where to Go

Traditionally, almost all waterfowlers have hunted on private land owned by clubs with hunting privileges handed down from generation to generation. Some waterfowlers are still lucky enough to belong to such a club, or to have inherited a good hunting spot from their waterfowling ancestors. Today, however, though private duck hunting clubs and groups that band together to buy or lease private property for hunting still exist, the scene is rapidly changing. For one thing, a good blind can rent for up to $2,000 a season, so many hunters are excluded from the sport. Additionally, land is being gobbled up at an alarming rate. Even "unusable" or "waste" land—that is, swamps and marshes—is bought up, drained, and filled, and this practice is eliminating many of yesterday's fine duck marshes.

The answer for many hunters is public hunting land under state and federal management. Although this is regulated hunting, these areas do give all hunters an equal chance, and also provide some extremely fine hunting.

An alternative is to scout around independently for a place to hunt.

Most waterfowling is still done on private land owned or leased by duck hunting clubs or groups of hunters.

This, too, is a challenge and can reward the diligent waterfowler with unusual and profitable spots, some practically in your own back yard.

HUNTING FEDERAL LANDS

The federal government owns about one-third of the land in the United States. Much of this land is in public use parks, national forests, national wilderness areas; and a great deal of it is also in waterfowl refuges. There are 289 national wildlife refuges scattered across the United States; 220 of these—making up over 2,589,292 acres of water and land—are managed primarily for waterfowl. Most of these refuges, ranging from small parcels of land to vast complexes of marsh, are operated by the fish and game departments of the various states in cooperation with the Department of the Interior. (Hunter dollars, through waterfowling stamps and excise taxes, are paying the way for many of these areas.)

Waterfowl refuges are constructed to protect migrating birds and offer rest along the flyways. These refuges are largely responsible for having brought waterfowl populations back to the numbers that exist today. Often a successful habitat attracts more waterfowl than it can effectively support. Hunting is important in these environments not only as a popular sport but as a necessary management control. The restric-

ADVANTAGES OF PUBLIC HUNTING AREAS

Some of the finest waterfowling in the country is found in the huge public hunting areas managed primarily for waterfowling.

Most public hunting areas have easy access points to enable the hunter to launch a boat. Some areas also rent boats and decoys.

Waterfowl refuges are skillfully managed to provide natural shelters and nesting areas that attract large flocks of birds and encourage breeding.

To some degree, birds are held in the area by supplies of food. Many of these areas are "worked" in agreement with local farmers, who put out crops such as corn. The refuge leaves its share standing while the farmer harvests his own. The results make for some of the finest shooting and best-tasting birds in the country.

In certain public hunting areas the regulations are pretty stiff and require that you hunt only from a specific blind.

tions which hunters observe also help to maintain the balance between waterfowl populations and the habitat that exists for them.

Some prime hunting spots that have become famous with waterfowlers are Swan Lake National Wildlife Refuge near Sumner, Missouri; Horicon Marsh near Madison, Wisconsin; and Horseshoe Lake, Illinois. These refuges sometimes have as many as 300,000 ducks and geese in residence during prime hunting season, and to control an area of, say, 20,000 acres and 300,000 waterfowl, it takes expert managers growing lots of food. Certain refuges have such fine habitat that they now serve as nesting areas for native flocks of geese and ducks. Some, in fact, are responsible for the fantastic comeback of the Giant Canada goose, a subspecies of Canada which was once almost extinct. As flocks of various birds build, populations often begin to overcrowd an area—then hunting seasons are opened on a species that, perhaps, was only recently very rare.

The states, too, like the federal government, have created some excellent waterfowl refuges. Some states have simply set aside marshland; others have built and studiously managed complex systems of pools, lakes, and streams. There are presently millions of acres of public waterfowl hunting grounds, and if we hunters continue to do our part to increase waterfowl nesting, feeding, and resting areas, then we will benefit from the resulting hunting areas as well.

The management of public hunting areas differs a great deal from state to state. In Arkansas, for example, you can simply walk in and hunt such refuges as the Bayou Meto, which covers 35,000 acres and is 7 miles wide and 15 miles long. But you better have a compass and a good map of the area, or you may not walk out. Other areas, such as Swan Lake or Schell-Osage in the neighboring state of Missouri, are much more restrictive. They require advance reservations, and you must arrive early in the morning, draw for a blind, then pay a fee for using it.

Hunting the public areas does require some different techniques, since you will be competing with a lot of other shooters. This can be very frustrating at times, but it can also be extremely challenging and rewarding. You must know the area thoroughly and practice sound hunting techniques. It also helps to have a few extra "tricks" in your bag to be consistently successful in public areas.

First, and most important, is to call properly. A good caller can get ducks in a crowded spot.

Second, get into an area before you hunt it, and find out where the ducks are. This technique is essential for any kind of hunting, but for some reason very few waterfowl hunters follow it, even though they may practice it religiously when hunting other game. Use binoculars if you have them and watch for feeding and resting ducks. It doesn't do any good to put out a great set of blocks and to call perfectly if all the ducks in the area are too far away for this to be effective.

Naturally, weekday hunting is the best. But—hint number three—if you can hunt only on weekends, forget about getting up in the middle of the night to be out for the early morning flight. Wait and go at about 8:30 or 9:30 A.M. Most of the ducks that have been out feeding will just be returning by then, and many of the early hunters will already have gone home. This brings up another good point: you should not only know *where* the ducks are feeding, but also *when*.

A technique we all know about but sometimes forget is that of picking up any shiny or bright objects in the area, including spent shot shells. Cover boat or blind numbers or any other light objects with wet burlap sacks.

Decoys must be set out properly. Many hunters set them too far from their blind. Arrange the outer fringes of your decoys no more than 35 or 40 yards out and leave an open pocket right in front of you. Ducks don't like to sit down in a crowded landing strip, so leave them an open space inside a large set of blocks. And avoid setting up a blind with the wind in your face. Since ducks invariably land upwind, your position should permit them to come in from left or right, not directly over you, but always angled away.

In timber you'll need only a dozen decoys; but if you're hunting open water in a heavily used public area, 75 decoys aren't too many, and many successful refuge hunters use over 100 decoys even on small inland lakes.

As long as ducks keep coming, don't shoot, unless they flare or turn away. You'll be surprised at how close they will come. And remember, with your outer decoys set at 35 to 40 yards, you have established a good killing range. Don't shoot at any ducks unless they come in over your decoys.

Most public hunting grounds are large, vast areas of brush as well as open water, and a good retrieving dog will more than double your chances of retrieving cripples. In most refuges, retrieving dogs are more than welcome; but make sure you check before taking them in.

Because public hunting areas tend to get crowded, honor the nearby hunters and don't try to call ducks away from them if the birds have already "set their wings" to go into their decoys.

For information on these waterfowling areas, write the individual state game and fish departments (the addresses of the various departments are listed in the Appendix).

In addition to these areas, some excellent public hunting land exists around the huge Corps of Engineers flood-control dams that are scattered across the United States. Ask or write your state Corps of Engineers office for information and regulations on these areas.

OTHER HUNTING GROUNDS

In hunting, but particularly in waterfowling, the hardest part of the hunt is finding a place! Nevertheless, hunters always overlook some good spots right in their own back yards. All you need is a little effort and imagination to turn them up.

Many smaller cities have community lakes for water supply and similar functions. Frequently, these areas can be hunted with permission from the area managers, who will usually let hunters put up a semipermanent blind as long as it is removed at the end of the season.

Private ponds and some lakes require only permission from their owners to hunt, as do many private duck clubs and duck blinds on private lakes.

Some pretty exciting hunting also awaits the hunter who shoots farm

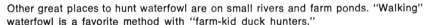
Other great places to hunt waterfowl are on small rivers and farm ponds. "Walking" waterfowl is a favorite method with "farm-kid duck hunters."

ponds or potholes. This is stalking at its best, requiring a great deal of patience, a tolerance for crawling in the mud, and a good knowledge of the ponds in your area. If possible, scan the pond first with binoculars. Locate the ducks and determine their species and sex. This is important with today's point system on waterfowl, and once you jump up and surprise the ducks you may not have time for proper identification. Plan your strategy. If you've laid your plan out well, in most cases you can circle a pond and come up on the dam side without too much crawling.

Pond jump shooting can afford plenty of surprises. A couple of years ago, my dad and I spotted about a half dozen mallards on a neighbor's pond. We made a good sneak up the pond dam, and on signal raised up to shoot. When we raised above the dam not 6 but 100 ducks came off the pond, and in the confusion neither of us collected a single one. We still can't figure how that many ducks were hidden in the cattails and millet around the pond's edge!

If you live near the ocean or even large inland lakes, you've got all

When scouting for your own waterfowling areas, there are many factors to look for. A good hunter knows what kinds of ducks and geese use what kinds of habitat in his area. Here the shallow water, and the abundance of cover and food plants, bullrushes, arrowhead, duckweed, etc., indicate this is a good location for puddle ducks such as mallards.

the hunting you'll need, although you'll have to know more about a larger variety of ducks. Duck hunting in these waters is traditionally rough and rugged, and takes good seamanship, knowledge of the water, and good rugged equipment to get you there and back. You'll also require specialized equipment such as sneakboxes, or other small "shooting boats" that can be towed behind larger transportation boats.

Some of the best duck and goose hunting to be had is on rivers and small creeks. If you want to get ducks early in the season, or late in the season when most open waters have frozen over, try slipping down a small river or creek in a camouflaged canoe or boat. Drifting quietly down a stream to ambush a duck dinner is a real challenge—one that will infect even the most blasé woodsman with a bad case of duck fever. You never quite know what lies around the next bend. Ducks like to relax on the calm backwaters and eddies on the inside of a bend, so when you approach a bend, pull close to the bank on the inside and slip around quietly. But be alert; you may drift within a few feet of sitting ducks. Several years ago, a friend and I discovered that early in the season turtles sometimes "stand watch" for the ducks in a small stream. When we rounded a bend and saw sunning turtles slide off their logs into the water, we often heard ducks leaving the area long before they could actually see us.

In hunting rivers, watch for signs of abandoned river channels. Often these old sloughs or oxbows provide some terrific hunting.

In most states, navigable rivers can be hunted by anyone; but do check your state game laws on ducks or geese before hunting the rivers. And remember that it's unlawful to hunt waterfowl from a boat with the motor running in all states, although some states allow you to pursue cripples in this manner.

There are two excellent ways to find lesser known hunting spots in your area. The first, and cheapest, is to buy a good topographical map. This will indicate sloughs, ponds, lakes, rivers, and so on, and can be used to find promising spots. All you have to do is locate the owners of the areas, who are listed in the county recorder's office. Ask them for permission to hunt or get a lease granting you hunting privileges.

The second good way to locate productive hunting, particularly on farm ponds, is to hire an airplane for a 1-hour ride. From the air you can spot hundreds of ponds, potholes, and sloughs you would never locate on the ground.

One final note: No matter where you hunt on private land, always make sure you first get permission from the owner of the land.

Appendix:
U.S. Conservation Departments

A list of the names and addresses of the fifty U.S. Conservation Departments follows. These departments will be able to furnish you with explicit information on the hunting areas within each state, such as conditions, types of waterfowl available, terrain, blind and boat rentals, and licenses. They can also give you information on the size of the hunting area, its open seasons, and the number of hunters easily accommodated. If you know you want to hunt in a specific area, contact that department for advance information, which should be most helpful.

Alabama

Department of Conservation
Division of Game and Fish
64 N. Union St.
Montgomery 36104

Alaska

Department of Conservation
Subport Bldg.
Juneau 99801

Arizona

Game and Fish Department
2222 W. Greenway
Phoenix 85007

Arkansas

Game and Fish Commission
State Capitol Grounds
Little Rock 72201

California
Department of Fish and Game
1416 9th St.
Sacramento 95814

Colorado
Game, Fish and Parks Division
6060 Broadway
Denver 30216

Connecticut
Board of Fisheries and Game
State Office Building
Hartford 06115

Delaware
Division of Fish and Wildlife
"D" Street
Dover 19901

Florida
Division of Game and Fresh Water
    Fish
620 So. Meridian
Tallahassee 32304

Georgia
State Game and Fish Commission
Trinity-Washington Bldg.
270 Washington St., S.W.
Atlanta 30334

Hawaii
Division of Fish and Game
530 So. Hotel St.
Honolulu 96813

Idaho
Fish and Game Department
Box 23
Boise 83707

Illinois
Department of Conservation
102 State Office Bldg.
400 So. Spring St.
Springfield 62706

Indiana
Department of Natural Resources
Division of Fish and Game
607 State Office Bldg.
Indianapolis 46209

Iowa
State Conservation Commission
State Office Bldg.
300 4th St.
Des Moines 50319

Kansas
Forestry, Fish and Game Commission
Box 1028
Pratt 67124

Kentucky
Department of Fish and Wildlife
    Resources
State Office Building Annex
Frankfort 40601

Louisiana
Wildlife and Fisheries Commission
400 Royal St.
New Orleans 70130

Maine
Department of Inland Fisheries and
    Game
State House
Augusta 04330

Maryland
Fish and Wildlife Administration
State Office Bldg.
Annapolis 21401

Massachusetts
Division of Fisheries and Game
100 Cambridge St.
Boston 02202

Michigan
Department of Natural Resources
Mason Bldg.
Lansing 48926

Minnesota
Division of Game and Fish
Department of Conservation
Centennial Bldg.
658 Cedar St.
St. Paul 55101

Mississippi
Game and Fish Commission
Game and Fish Bldg.
402 High St.
Box 451
Jackson 39205

Missouri
Department of Conservation
Box 180
Jefferson City 65101

Montana
Fish and Game Department
Helena 59601

Nebraska
Nebraskaland
State Capitol Bldg.
Lincoln 68509

Nevada
Department of Fish and Game
Box 10678
Reno 89510

New Hampshire
Fish and Game Department
34 Bridge St.
Concord 03301

New Jersey
Division of Fish, Game and
  Shell Fisheries
Box 1809
Trenton 08625

New Mexico
Department of Game and Fish
State Capitol
Santa Fe 87501

New York
Division of Fish and Wildlife
State Dept. of Environmental
  Conservation
50 Wolf Rd.
Campus, Albany 12226

North Carolina
Wildlife Resources Commission
Box 2919
Raleigh 27602

North Dakota
State Game and Fish Department
2121 Lovell Ave.
Bismarck 58501

Ohio
Department of Natural Resources
Division of Wildlife
1500 Dublin Rd.
Columbus 43212

Oklahoma
Department of Wildlife Conservation
1801 No. Lincoln
Oklahoma City 73105

Oregon
State Game Commission
Box 3503
Portland 97208

Pennsylvania
Game Commission
P.O. Box 1567
Harrisburg 17120

Rhode Island
Department of Natural Resources
Veteran's Memorial Bldg.
Providence 02903

South Carolina
Wildlife Resources Department
1015 Main St.
Box 167
Columbus 29202

South Dakota
Department of Game, Fish and Parks
State Office Bldg.
Pierre 57501

Tennessee
Game and Fish Commission
Box 40747
Ellington Center
Nashville 37220

Texas
Parks and Wildlife Department
John H. Reagan Bldg.
Austin 78701

Utah
Division of Fish and Game
1596 W.N. Temple
Salt Lake City 84116

Vermont
Fish and Game Department
151 Main St.
Montpelier 05602

Virginia
Commission of Game and Inland
    Fisheries
4010 W. Broad St.
Box 11104
Richmond 23230

Washington
Department of Game
600 No. Capitol Way
Olympia 98501

West Virginia
Department of Natural Resources
1800 Washington St.
Charleston 25305

Wisconsin
Department of Natural Resources
Box 450
Madison 53701

Wyoming
Game and Fish Commission
Box 1589
Cheyenne 83001

Index

Credits

2 Browning Arms.
3 (*bottom*) Kentucky Department of Fish and Wildlife.
6 Michigan Department of Natural Resources.
8 (*top*) Michigan Department of Natural Resources.
13 (*top*) Virginia Commission of Game and Inland Fisheries.
13 (*bottom*) Michigan Department of Natural Resources.
19 Wisconsin Natural Resources Department.
24 (*top*) Virginia Commission of Game and Inland Fisheries.
25 (*top*) Virginia Commission of Game and Inland Fisheries.
26 Kentucky Department of Fish and Wildlife.
31 (*top*) Missouri Department of Conservation.
37 (*middle left*) Missouri Department of Conservation.
38–41 Department of the Interior, Fish and Wildlife Service.
79 (*middle*) Missouri Department of Conservation.
84 Kentucky Department of Fish and Wildlife.
102 Herter's, Inc.
106 (*bottom*) Wisconsin Conservation Department.
111 Missouri Department of Conservation.
113 Orvis Company.
124 (*top*) Old Town Canoe Co.
124 (*bottom*) Kentucky Fish and Wildlife Department.
125 Old Town Canoe Co.
129 Herter's, Inc.
130 (*top*) Grumman Co.
131 Oklahoma Fish and Game Department.
133 Browning Arms.
134 Browning Arms.
136 Browning Arms.
157 Virginia Commission of Game and Inland Fisheries.
159 (*top*) Wisconsin Natural Resources Department.
160 Sporting Dog Specialties, Inc.
174 Georgia Department of Natural Resources.
176 Eddie Bauer, Inc.
180 (*left*) Jon-e Hand Warmers
181 (*top*) Eddie Bauer, Inc.
186 (*top*) Hageman Company.
195 Missouri Department of Conservation.
197 Missouri Department of Conservation.
200 (*bottom*) Ducks Unlimited.
204 Missouri Department of Conservation.
205 (*top*) Missouri Department of Conservation.
205 (*middle*) Arkansas Game and Fish Commission.
205 (*bottom*) Missouri Department of Conservation.
210 (*bottom right*) Michigan Department of Natural Resources.